Wakefield Press

The Long Way Home

Lydia Laube was born on her family's farm in the mid-north of South Australia. She was blessed (or cursed) at birth by a passing fairy, who left her with itchy feet and insatiable curiosity. After completing nursing qualifications in Adelaide, she crammed her belongings in a VW beetle and set off to see the world. In twenty-five years of nursing, Lydia has delivered babies on her knees in New Guinea, tended clinics in dug-out canoes in Papua, worked on a junk in the Hong Kong harbour, served the poor in the slums of Naples and flown with the Australian flying doctor service. Her first book, *Behind the Veil*, describing her adventures in Saudi Arabia, has been an Australian best-seller.

Lydia Laube, when she is not travelling, divides her time between Adelaide and Darwin.

T0359716

The Long Way Home
'Nobody goes *that* way'

LYDIA LAUBE

Wakefield Press

Wakefield Press
1 The Parade West
Kent Town
South Australia 5067
www.wakefieldpress.com.au

First published August 1994
Reprinted December 1994, 2002, 2009.

Design by Ann Wojczuk
Cover design by Bill Farr
Typeset by Clinton Ellicott
Printed and bound by Hyde Park Press, Adelaide

National Library of Australia Cataloguing-in-Publication entry

Laube, Lydia, 1948– .
The long way home.

ISBN-13: 978 1 86254 325 6
ISBN-10: 1 86254 325 9

1. Laube, Lydia, 1948–   – Journeys. 2. Saudi Arabia –
Description and travel. 3. Egypt – Description and travel.
4. Sudan – Description and travel. 5. Kenya – Description
and travel. 6. India – Description and travel. I. Title.

915.04

Government
of South Australia

Arts SA

To the memory of my father

Contents

1 Boomerang!

Twenty thousand feet above the Himalayas, entombed in the bowels of a jumbo jet, is no place to change your mind about your destination. Given the chance, though, I would have absconded with the greatest alacrity. Daft I had been to venture into Saudi Arabia when it was an unknown quantity, but stark raving mad I must be to be returning.

When I had left Medina, supposedly on leave, but quite sure it was for good, the company employing me had given me a return ticket to Australia and back. From the complacent safety of Adelaide, it had seemed a waste not to use it. Air tickets to the Middle East are very expensive and I wanted to visit Egypt again. There was also the matter of the large amount of money the company still owed me.

My six weeks at home had flashed by and, before I had really thought about it, the date on my return ticket had arrived. It was time to go. And I did. Time had softened the memory of the deprivation of my exiled life outside the walls of Medina, Islam's second holiest city.

Before I departed Adelaide I phoned the company administrator in Saudi Arabia to discover my destination. He said I was to go to Mustafa Khalid bin Rachman, the other hospital they managed at Medina, which had been left suddenly without a nursing director. Horrified, I reminded him of the promised transfer elsewhere than Medina. He replied that it would only be for a little while, that they would transfer me elsewhere as soon as a replacement could be found, and that I could leave at any time if I did not like it. So I agreed.

I looked around the plane. Saudia's international aircraft were the latest models and obviously designed to convince the world of Saudi Arabia's affluence. At the check-in counter in Singapore I had been upgraded to first class. It seemed to be the practice to do this if there were vacant seats and the few Europeans who fly with Saudia were usually given these in order to impress them. Saudia appears to have an inferiority complex about its 'dry' status – the reason most Europeans give it a miss – so it tries to make up for this failing by supplying every other possible luxury. They succeeded. I *was* impressed.

My seat was an enormous lounge chair and my neighbour a genuine, original sheik. He had swept aboard, long white *thobe* swishing around his soft camel-leather sandals, dark brown camel-hair cloak trimmed with gold braid flowing impressively behind him, and the traditional red and white checked *gutera* on his head. Finding me there alone was obviously a shock, but he quickly recovered his composure, *salaammed* and greeted me courteously. His secretary, who was billeted in tourist class with the common herd, and only ventured now and then into our rarefied company, told me that my companion was the Sheik Anwar bin Kalim al Suddah and that he was a great leader of the people of the Western Desert.

Sheik Anwar said, 'I have been to Singapore to see my younger sons. They are studying at the university.'

'How many?' I asked.

'Three,' he replied, 'the others are in London.'

I wondered how many others there were, but felt it might be exceeding the limits of courtesy to enquire. I asked him whether he had any horses, knowing that was a safe bet, and we talked about them instead, a subject we both found interesting.

'You may come and ride my horses one day,' he offered kindly.

'*En shal'lah*,' I replied, 'God willing.'

But we both knew that I could not.

The flight was bumpy for most of the nine hours of its duration and, white knuckle flyer that I am, this made me twitchy, but I consoled myself with the fabulous food, which even included caviar.

On arrival at Riyadh at eight in the evening, I found that I had missed the last flight to Medina – despite the excellence of their airline, Saudia still had not been able to eliminate the Arab lack of interest in timetables – and I was forced to spend the night in the airport. I wasn't able to leave without someone claiming and acknowledging receipt of me. The male desk staff most courteously suggested that I should avail myself of the 'Women's Room' for the night and directed me to it. I had fears that it might be the same place in which I had been detained on my previous arrival. I did not want any reminders of that unpleasant experience when I had been unceremoniously shunted into a room, also designated 'Women's Room', and given into the charge of two huge female chaperones covered entirely in black cloth. Convinced I had been arrested, but with no idea why, I had been almost panic stricken, but had practised eastern calm for an interminable time until eventually released into the care of the company representative.

I discovered later that I had caused such consternation

because I was alone. A woman cannot be responsible for herself in Saudi Arabia. She has no separate identity, but is always merely the appendage of a male.

My lack of a husband, that essential accessory, had sorely hindered me. At times I had longed for a husband. Anybody's.

This time I had no problems about being alone. I had an ongoing ticket to Medina and my work and residency papers to prove that I was not a loose woman, and before the plane landed I had done as the old hands do, donned my *abeya* – the all-enveloping black shroud – and wrapped my head and neck in a long black scarf. At first in Saudi I had hated the scarves and the dreary black *abeya*, but after a few months had accepted them as normal dress.

This time the Women's Room was somewhere else entirely, praise Allah for the Muslim protection of women. There was a special spot provided for our species so that we did not have the discomfort of waiting in the public lounge under the gaze of men. The room was large and air-conditioned and furnished with all manner of comforts. There were couches, tables, chairs, four divan beds and a large adjoining bathroom with toilets and showers. I was the only occupant. I made myself comfortable, lying down on a divan in all my clothes and covering myself with my *abeya*. It was not possible to turn off the lights – another precaution taken to protect us – so I put my scarf over my face, and went to sleep.

I was awakened at dawn by the call to prayer and found I had been joined some time in the night by two ladies who were now performing their ritual ablutions noisily in the bathroom. After this, they took down the prayer mats, which were kept rolled up on a bench when not in action, faced them to Mecca and proceeded to pray. I stayed under my veil and feigned sleep. It is a grave offence for a non-believer to interfere with the faithful at prayer.

The first plane to Medina left at seven and I was on it, arriving about an hour and a half later. I was met by the hospital administrator and head of the company at Mustafa Khalid bin Rachman, Abdul Aizzat, an urbanely-spoken, swarthy type. I learned later that he was a Palestinian with friends in high places. He had one glaring fault, a very serious one for this country. He was over-fond of feminine company. Considering his appearance, which was reminiscent of a good-natured but homely frog (he was short, fat, pear-shaped, popeyed and had warts) he did not have a lot of success with his overtures, but he tried, oh, how he tried. I learned never to be alone in his office with him. Even with the door open, he could still manage to grope for your leg under the desk.

A nursing staff guard of honour had been mustered the evening before and herded to the airport in a Ministry of Health bus to greet me. They had lost their enthusiasm when I failed to materialise and had not reappeared. I did not mind. I was feeling a bit too jaded for a welcome committee.

The gates swung shut behind the car and the barricade was lowered. The guard with the rifle resumed his vigil. We drove to the entrance of the harem where another armed guard waited in his sentry box. I was back. Not only in Saudi Arabia, but in Medina, the sands of which I had sworn would never again see the imprint of my dainty sandals.

2 Back behind the veil

Just over a year ago I had come to King Fahid hospital, my first place of employment in the kingdom, an 'innocent abroad', despite all the travelling I had done.

I had answered an advertisement for nurses in the *Sydney Morning Herald*, and been hired by a 'headhunter' recruiting for one of the many companies managing hospitals and other facilities in the Middle East. All Saudi hospitals are run on a contract basis. There are no qualified Saudi staff, so they hire a company, usually from Britain, Europe or the United States, to provide staff and management for them. The company then employs a recruiter to find the staff; senior nurses from the west – the UK, USA and Australia; and junior from India, the Philippines, Pakistan, Korea and neighbouring Arab countries such as Egypt. Whether the company you are sent to work for is good or bad is a gamble and, unless you can obtain inside information (the recruiter is not likely to tell you, all he wants is the money he gets for delivering your body), the truth can come as a nasty shock when it is too late. Mine was a Lebanese and Palestinian owned company run by a gang of black-hearted villains, and was almost as bad as they come.

The recruiters had never visited the hospital 'without the walls' of Medina. I had been the first Australian to work at this site and one of only a handful of westerners, none of whom would have been inside Medina. To breach the walls of the holy city – the burial place of the Prophet Mohommed – is forbidden on pain of death to non-believers. The road to the hospital skirts widely around the city, to protect it from contamination by even the eyes of the infidels employed there.

At King Fahid hospital I had been dumped in a great cell block of female accommodation and left to fend alone in a huge, filthy, broken-down flat where nothing worked except me. *I* was slave-driven ten or more hours a day, six days a week. In the promised self-contained, fully-equipped flat there were no linen, towels, crockery or cutlery. I cleaned, repaired and equipped my quarters, then took on the hospital, which was Alcatraz itself: a great, gaunt cement blot on the horizon, jumping with cockroaches big enough to throw a saddle over, riddled with medical malpractice, and booby-trapped with pit-falls for the unwary. Its corridors were landmined with possible sins against Islam. Battling indifference and ignor-ance at work, as much from the company as from the Ministry of Health, which owned the hospital, and living a socially-deprived existence, I survived to complete my contract a year later. Battered but triumphant, I had fled rejoicing, but not before the company had blackmailed me into signing for another dose of perdition. 'But not here in Medina', I had stressed over and over before I put my mark on their paper, 'anywhere but here!'

Well, *here* I was.

Mustafa (hospital) Khalid bin Rachman, two kilometres down the road from King Fahid, was very different, but was another prison nevertheless. This cage was a little more gilded, but just as dirty. It had been built three years earlier by a group of wealthy businessmen to cater for those rich enough to pay for its luxurious private facilities. The hospital hadn't prospered, had been taken over by the government, and was now being run by the Ministry of Health which, knowing no better, had given its management contract to Omega, the management company from hell.

The housing was arranged in three separate sections: male, female, and married. Each section had a large paved courtyard with a swimming pool in the middle, three-storeyed buildings and covered concrete walkways. The married quarters consisted of villas equipped with every possible amenity, even a spa, each bedroom having an adjoining sitting room and bathroom. The previous incumbent of my post had been male, qualified in England and anglicised, but Arab by birth and Arabic-speaking. His position as a director of a department had entitled him to be housed in a villa, and I should have been too, but this threw the powers-that-be into a quandary. There had been no previous female head of department, and they did not know what to do with me. They feared for public morals if they allowed me to live alone in a villa in the married quarters; this would be like putting the pigeon among the cats. Wives had their husbands to protect them from the advances of other men. The previous nursing director had been trusted to live as a single person among the wives because their husbands could protect them from him, but who would protect me from the husbands? It did not occur to them that I might be able to protect myself. I was only a poor, weak, submissive female. So I was sent to rough it with the single females in their compound.

If it's possible to believe, the female staff here were even more confined and restricted than at the King Fahid hospital. Their housing was well-distanced from the other two sections and surrounded by a high wall with only one gate, where an armed guard reposed in his sentry box twenty-four hours a day. On one side of the harem the inmates could look over the wall and see the main gate, fifty metres away, with its entrance barred by more guards with rifles – not a cheery sight.

I was given a 'bachelor' apartment: a sitting room and a bedroom with en suite bathroom, separated by a small space which had to function as a kitchen and dining room. It was nicely furnished, with ultra-modern equipment and fittings. I was very comfortable, except that the bars on the windows made me feel like a captured bird. The main room had a heavy wooden lattice over its large picture window, that could not be lifted or moved, and through which I had to view the world. Once again I had been forced to surrender my passport on arrival, and this left me feeling insecure and isolated. It was very hard to return to this kind of life after my taste of freedom. At least this time, however, I knew that it would not be for long; and the reception given me – I was allowed a day to rest before going to the hospital – and the conditions, were a vast improvement on those at King Fahid.

In lieu of my passport I was given a piece of paper, one side in Arabic and the other in English, stating who I was, for whom I worked, and that my employer was responsible for me. This paper had to be on my person at all times, but as few officials read Arabic well and almost none read English, it never proved to be much help in times of drama.

Above me lived two heavily-built, jolly Egyptian technicians, Alfat, wonderfully well-named, and Fifi, who loved to whoop it up at all hours of the night, dancing to the wail of Middle Eastern music. Sometimes I accepted an invitation to join them and they taught me a little of the art of belly dancing, but otherwise I would go to bed wearing ear plugs when the air-conditioner was not on to drown the noise.

There was even a chance for exercise. Not that I am normally fond of undue exertion – I think running about the roadsides and getting red in the face is most unbecoming and not a little unsafe – but some gentle flexion of the muscles in a swimming pool is quite in order. Every night I swam in the pool after dusk. There is something gorgeously sensual about swimming in the dark, gliding through shimmering tepid water. Unfortunately this pursuit only lasted until the end of November. Then the temperature dropped below thirty-eight degrees Celsius, it was declared to be winter, and the pool was cleaned, emptied and put away in mothballs until next summer.

The company bus took the company staff on shopping trips to the village *souk* for about an hour each week, and there was one trip to Jeddah or Yanbu, *en shal'lah*, God willing, each month. Occasionally, instead of the village, we visited the Tabuk Road *souk*, a row of open iron sheds on an arid, empty road providing goods for the pilgrims. They sold pots and pans, glassware, tinware and a large assortment of awful plastic plates.

The compound grounds and buildings were a great change from the institutional, utilitarian, concrete jungle of King Fahid hospital. The general appearance of the complex was neat and pleasing, in green and white. The hospital was beautiful, with open spaces and tiled floors making it cool and airy. The walls and ceilings were white and the columns and staircases lime green. There were fountains, pools, palm trees and shrubs at the hospital entrance and in the courtyards between the various wings, which were reached via covered, colonnaded walkways of white stucco. The wards were on the three upper storeys, while the offices, X-ray department and other facilities were on the ground floor and in the basement. There was even a snack bar for visitors and patients.

An attractively rounded, pale greenish-blue mosque with a very tall white minaret was just inside the gate. It was surrounded by small, dense palm trees planted in squares in the white concrete. Behind the minaret loomed, brooding and dark, a line of ancient, bare rock, flat-topped mountains, standing sentinel against a sky that was almost always a blazing blue.

The hospital had 260 beds and 120 Ministry of Health nursing staff, not nearly enough to cover all the wards and departments. The company had sixty staff members, mostly expatriate Egyptians, Sudanese and Indians. This was a big improvement on the number of company staff at King Fahid hospital and made life a lot easier. Fourteen of the company staff were European: English, Scottish, Irish and Canadian. Unfortunately there were only seven company nursing staff. The Ministry of Health nurses were mostly Filipinas with a sprinkling of people of other Asian nationalities. There were quite a few Egyptians and a handful of other Arabs from surrounding countries, such as Palestine. Only three of the seven company nursing staff were European, two of whom left after six weeks and only one more, a male nurse, came – and went – very quickly, after suffering a nervous collapse.

The one remaining European staff member I was blessed with was as much use as a pork chop at a Jewish festival. Out of her depth, disoriented, probably deranged, Sister Olive was an arrogant and gross middle-aged English-woman who looked like a badly-worn, overstuffed sofa. She gave every appearance of having been shovelled hastily into her pants and jacket by a tipsy grave digger.

She was supposedly a nursing supervisor, but did little except plod about, leaning forward to peer intently at the face of anyone to whom she spoke. Even the Bedu, laced with bandoliers of bullets, ran at the sight of her. She gabbled very fast in a strong north-country accent that no one understood. This made her savage, and she would shout, thinking that a raised voice equalled increased comprehension. When it didn't, she would give up and stamp off in a huff.

One day the company engineer told me how he had sent a Sudanese workman to do repairs in the flat Sister Olive shared with two company radiographers. The harem guard escorted him to the door and, thinking no one was there, the Sudanese man entered alone. Suddenly, Sister Olive swept into the passageway and came towards him like a ship in full sail, huge, lily-white and just about naked. She was in her bathers. The engineer said the poor workman was still shaking with shock an hour and a half after the confrontation.

I encountered my first hurdle, the Saudi hospital director. Although a doctor, he had qualified and worked only in Egypt and Saudi. He spoke little English and was dead against the idea of a female director of nursing, especially a European. Apparently he was convinced I would not be able to handle the job and would behave in a superior and demanding fashion. His contact with western women had been limited and, judging by his attitude, those he had met must have been horrible specimens. He was determined to send me home immediately without setting eyes on me or giving me a chance. This did not seem such a bad idea to me either but, obstreperous creature that I am, I wanted the opportunity to prove him wrong. Abdul Aizzat, the company administrator, spoke to him at length and persuaded him to at least let me try. I decided to ignore his attitude and get on with the job in my usual way. If he did not like that, too bad: I did not want to stay longer than it took to squeeze my money out of Omega.

I was taken into his sumptuous office at last, and found him to be a very large, rather gentle man, civilised and chivalrous. The penny dropped! He did not think a woman could be tough enough to cope with the task of running the nursing service of his hospital. To him women were fragile, defenceless beings. I wasn't about to disillusion him. I needed all the protection I could get to survive in this country.

Behaving in the best Arab manner, I waited to be spoken to, sitting with eyes cast down. The administrator said, 'Doctor Ibrahim, this is Sister Lydia'.

I greeted him, 'A Salama lecum,' calling Allah's peace down upon his head.

He had no option but to reply with the response, 'A le cum a salam' ('And on you also be peace').

I kept my feet together on the floor, my hands clasped in my lap, and said little.

After I had completed my first inspection of the hospital, I flopped down at my desk in despair. The task was daunting. Behind its glamorous façade, the hospital was as filthy as King Fahid hospital and the nursing care looked even worse. The wards and pantries were dirty, food was scattered on the floors – to the delight of the resident army of cockroaches who reigned triumphant over all – the fridges were putrid, and everywhere doors opened on foul toilets. The bins overflowed, the door handles were covered with grease. There was dirt on the walls, stairways, rails and bed trolleys and the whole mess was topped off by a generous sprinkling of cigarette butts. In the burns unit I found a small Indian woman casually waving a large feather duster along the cupboard tops like a magic wand, merrily showering all and sundry with micro-organisms. I watched technicians collect blood from patients and toss the dirty needles in open ward bins or on the floor.

It was a shame that, for all the company staff employed, so few had been found for nursing positions and none for housekeeping or cleaning supervision. No matter how many clerks, secretaries, engineers, laboratory and other technicians there are, they cannot greatly raise the standard of the ultimate purpose of the hospital – patient care. I was tempted merely to fill the director of nursing's chair and coast along until it was time to go, as the previous occupant had obviously done.

Discarding that idea, I set to work. The biggest hurdle was the Middle Ages mentality, which could see nothing wrong, for instance, with the male Arab assistant of the snack bar, a burning cigarette drooping from his lower lip, idly, languidly, combing his hair over the uncovered pita bread sandwiches. Sometimes, though, I was amused by the poetic justice in their way of doing things. Sadat Jamal, one of the Saudi administration staff, had an accident in his car and did considerable damage to the person and property of another Saudi. He was judged guilty and the offended party was allowed to sentence him. First on the long list of penance he was given was to abstain from smoking between dawn and dusk. For such a heavy smoker this was a real trial and he was worth avoiding from then on, as he became horribly grumpy without his nicotine fix every ten minutes.

After seeing the beauty and luxury of the hospital and buildings I had high hopes for that which might issue forth from the kitchen. I was monumentally disappointed. There on my plate to greet me was my old friend, the desiccated chicken, waving its scrawny leg at me and defying me to do my worst with the plastic knife and fork provided. The food was supplied by the same catering company that dispensed misfortune on a plate at King Fahid.

3 Perfectly useless

The hospital director summoned me to his office a week after I started and asked for a report on the condition of the hospital. I told him plainly that it was extremely dirty. He was livid, and demanded that I join him next morning for a hospital inspection tour; he was going to make me withdraw my statement.

Walking from ward to ward the next morning, I calmly pointed out to him each grotty area we passed. We got no further than the first floor before he called a halt to the inspection. He was furious, but this time with the cleaning supervisors and the heads of departments. He called a major council of war, and ranted and raved at them, telling them the place was an abomination. I wondered that he had not noticed it before. Turning to me he said, 'Sister, *you* will make it clean!'

Oh, no! What had I done? There were a director of cleaning services, several cleaning supervisors and a legion in the mop and bucket brigade. Why had I been stupid enough to mention the dirt?

There was nothing for it, however, but to enter into my new profession of Cleaning Lady Extraordinaire with a will. The company with the cleaning contract was Egyptian (that speaks for itself: 'Egyptian cleaner' is a contradiction in terms), so now I had the Egyptian Mafia gunning for me. Get rid of this meddlesome Kangaroo and it would be back to their nice comfortable lives of leisure, smoking and drinking tea all day with their chums in cosy offices. Blood was spilled before they took me seriously, saw that I really meant business and got their cleaners actually to do some cleaning.

The hospital director, feeling I needed moral support, appointed one Said Hamed as co-inspector of the clean-up. Said, a gigantically tall Sudanese, was softly spoken and benevolent, but slow - 'Slow Sid' I named him. He trailed around after me on one round, but by the second floor I had lost him, no doubt to his great relief as well as mine, and he never appeared on my rounds again.

The working conditions were less stressful, but the problems at Mustafa KBR were much the same as I had found at KFH, with lack of sufficient nurses heading the list. Incompetent nurses came next, then the lack of adequate supplies, orientation programs, fire drill, clinical instructors, inservice lectures, identity bands for patients, monitoring of X-ray levels on staff, and bed lists. There were no written hospital policies or procedures. The nursing staff, over-worked and under-quota as they were, were loaded with many non-nursing duties. The secretaries supplied to help on the wards did not speak, read or write English, which made them a hindrance. For example, they wrote the patients' menus in Arabic, and even nurses who spoke some Arabic couldn't read more than I could, which was only numbers and a few signs.

The linen service, run by another inefficient contract company, was in chaos. We could never find enough clean linen for the patients. I discovered later that it was being systematically stolen, spirited out by ingenious means, and sold in the Medina *souk*. At this time, however, the nurses were being accused of losing it. To spare the nurses the enormous time and effort they spent each day trying to find and account for linen, I set up a linen impress system. Everyone told me it would not work, but it did, and quite well too. As there was no one to whom tasks could be delegated – they were either untrustworthy or too busy – I took on the monumental task of counting and recording every piece of linen in the hospital.

At least I got my uniforms washed at this hospital. The delivery and retrieval system used by the delightful Pakistani man in charge of the operation was quaintly charming. I presented myself and my dirty uniforms to him and, after we exchanged salutations, he laboriously counted the uniforms and gave each individual item a number. He entered the numbers in a great Doomsday Book, painstakingly wrote a receipt in copperplate handwriting, and gave me a copy, without which redemption was impossible. My name was inscribed indelibly in large block letters across the back collar of my jackets, and each article was tagged by sewing on it a small square of linen bearing its number. Finally, the uniforms were consigned to the innards of an enormous cauldron from which they escaped in one piece only by a miracle. The process of presenting a uniform took about fifteen minutes, and it took almost as long to redeem it. The Keeper of the Uniforms provided a chair for those waiting, praise Allah.

Now that I had a reasonably clean hospital and enough clean linen for the beds, I tackled the matter of nursing care. What a bitter struggle! There was no communication between departments, wards, nurses or supervisors. I called a charge nurses' meeting to try to arrange regular meetings. No one arrived on time and half did not turn up at all. Everyone worked in their own small area of light, unhappy and apathetic, trying to ignore the darkness around them. When I had to do one nurse's end of year assessment, which decided whether or not she got an increase in salary, she did not even put in an appearance.

Once I had an altercation with a Palestinian male nurse. I tried to move him to another ward and he did not want to go. He threatened to complain about me to the Prince. I said, 'Do your worst.' He went to the hospital director instead, thinking he, as a fellow-Muslim and a male, would help him. To my surprise the director sent him packing and supported me.

The other hospital staff contained a few memorable characters. There was Yusef, ('useless'), a fat Egyptian, keeper of the stores, who was careful to live up to his name – it was like drawing teeth to persuade him to part with anything on his shelves. Then there was Mr Perfect, the Saudi bookkeeper, who was so pristinely beautiful and charming that all the girls swooned when he smiled at them. Me too.

The person who terrified me was the Ministry of Health director general, who came from Medina now and then to do spot inspections, usually accompanied by explosions and fearsome threats of punishment. One day he slapped a male Pakistani cleaner twice across the face because the bins had not been emptied. He was not a nice person and I dreaded his visits, thinking maybe I'd be next for a slapping.

At one stage I was sent six male student nurses from the recently established all-male school of nursing in Medina. They were supposed to be given supervised practice and work experience. This proved impossible. They refused to do anything menial, such as taking care of a patient, and spent all day smoking, chatting and drinking tea. (Getting in some good practice for being working Saudis.) I asked them through an interpreter what they *did* want to do. It turned out that they all wanted my job: to be the director of nursing as soon as they graduated. Training schools are supposed to be equipping Saudis to take over the running of hospitals and phasing out the need for foreign help. I think it will be a long time coming.

Some moments of humour were provided by the bulletins and memos that appeared daily on my desk. I was informed that one of the patients with a bad back had been placed in 'extraction' (that should fix him!). Another had a 'urinary catheter with a bigot attached' (to each his own) and repairs were needed on the 'patience trolleys' – you needed one of those if you were waiting in our Casualty. I read that the names on the 'rooster' had been changed because a nurse had the 'tootache' (there's nothing as bad as an aching toot). Some of the names on the 'rooster' were amusement themselves. I learned that I had in my charge Hitler, Mingy, Suparman, Abdul Rutin, Mate and Ruslin Rape.

One day when a patient had a cardiac arrest I discovered, hard though it is to believe, that there was no crash call system at all; no one seemed to have heard of CPR – cardiac pulmonary resuscitation. I borrowed someone from KFH to give lectures and we started practising. It was going quite well by the time I left, but I had the feeling that only the rehearsals were ever going to be successful. When it came to the real thing, panic took over and the routine shot through like a Bondi tram, to be replaced by a three-ring circus. Nurses would totally ignore someone really in need of restoring, and give vigorous mouth-to-mouth resuscitation to someone who was nowhere near dead. This proved irksome to the recipient, and they or their relatives were voluble in their condemnation.

I started some fire drill, but rescuers attempting to evacuate patients through fire exits encountered more locked doors than the Bank of England, somewhat marring the success of the exercise. I was also on a committee that was formulating a major disaster plan. As we ploughed our way through elaborate and convoluted schemes, I pictured the major disaster being the arrival of the hospital team.

And so I went on collecting jobs. I was now the fire officer, medical educator, housekeeper, cleaning supervisor and safety officer. The latter job made me aware of the hospital tradesmen's complete disregard, bordering on contempt, for anything resembling a safety code. I had a personal taste of the expertise of the electricians. I brought disaster down on my unsuspecting head one night in my flat by doing nothing more adventurous than removing the washing machine's electric plug from the wall socket. There was a deafening bang, out flew a great sheet of flame and all the lights went out, including mine, almost. I was thrown across the room and slammed into the wall. The next day the 'experts' and fixers demolished half the building while repairing the plug, and left me a note, written in felt pen on the white painted wall by my door, to say they had called. Arabia's first modern graffiti artists?

In the hospital wards, patients and diseases did not differ from those at KFH. Now that this was a Ministry of Health hospital, the main intake of patients were the Bedu – nomadic desert people who lead traditional tribal lives – and the towns-people of Medina. During the change of seasons we had an influx of patients suffering what was locally termed 'the common cold'. It was in fact most uncommon. The symptoms were high fever, severe headache, vomiting, diarrhoea and intense pains in the stomach, legs and back. If this was a common cold, what on earth could the flu be like?

I found the female patients gentle, ingenuous, and at times playfully roguish. In the women's wards, forbidden to men and guarded against their entry, I would often find groups sitting crosslegged on their beds, laughing and talking together. While relaxing like this most women still wore their *abeyas*, but they lifted their outer veils and threw them back over their heads. The boldest removed their head coverings altogether. Under the outer veil some wore a lesser veil. This was the type usually pictured by westerners, a piece of black cloth anchored over the bridge of the nose by strings tied at the back of the head.

Watching eyes flashing over this half-veil and observing the eloquent, and often elegant, movements of their small hands and wrists, I was reminded of something an Egyptian doctor once said to me, and understood at last what he had meant. When he first saw me wrapped in my *abeya*, with my black head scarf wound around my head and neck, he had said, 'Oh! Sister Lydia, you are beautiful in an *abeya*!' (They used the word 'beautiful' liberally in the Middle East, not always in its literal sense.)

Curious, I had asked him why he said this. It seemed to me, concealed as I was among a shapeless bundle of shrouds, that there was not enough visible on which to make a judgement. He explained that in *purdah*, where you saw only the hands and eyes, the rest was left to the imagination and therefore the possibilities were endless. I am still trying to work out if this was a compliment. Was he romantic or a realist?

The Beduin ladies could be quite whimsical on the subject of marriage. Matrimony in the Middle East is, for men, a fragile thing that can be easily dissolved. Merely to say, 'I divorce thee,' three times is enough. But this does not apply to women. Life without a husband was inconceivable for a Saudi woman. (It was even pretty difficult for a foreigner!) The women were fascinated by the fact that I had no husband and had, compared to them, unlimited freedom. They were free to venture out without a male relative only in circumscribed areas, such as the *souk* and the hospital. They could, with their dominant male's permission, visit these places during the day, but had to be heavily veiled and in the company of one or more other women. Asking them if they would like to be husbandless sent them into gales of giggles followed by choruses of '*Awah*' and '*Halas, halas*', which loosely translates as, 'You bet your bippy.'

Even discharging a female patient from the hospital was fraught with problems. If she did not have a husband *in situ* she could not be sent home until a male relative came to claim her. It was thought that she might be highjacked on the way home or run away with another man. (She might well have, if the penalties had not been so severe.) While she was consigned to its care, the hospital assumed the role of guardian and was responsible for her. The relative coming to collect her wrote his name on a form and she was released – signed, sealed and delivered, like a parcel.

After dark fell we were not allowed to let any female visitors remaining at the hospital leave without a male escort. The staff had to contact an acceptable relative to come and get them or, failing this, find them beds for the night. I was warned constantly about the dark and its dangers for women, but I was never personally conscious of being in peril. I always felt perfectly safe behind the big wall with its ever-present guard, who was armed to the teeth ready to repulse any would-be invaders seeking to make my acquaintance. The same applied to the hospital and the compound; I would have only had to raise the tiniest squeak for a battalion of protectors to pop up. I have no doubt that I was, in fact, watched carefully in case I was not averse to a possible invasion or had even decided to encourage some fraternisation. As for what might happen 'without the walls', I never got a chance to find out. On our few excursions outside, I was never left alone long enough to discover whether my charms were adequate to attract attention.

There were, however, one or two unfortunate incidents involving Filipina and other Asian nurses. I was advised that if it was necessary to transfer a patient to a hospital in Medina after dark I should always send male nurses as escorts in the ambulance or police car. If the patient was female and I had to send a female escort, I was told I must send two nurses, one to look after the patient and the other to look after her. Nurses escorting patients had in the past been attacked, molested and raped by drivers, patients and relatives, but the worst offenders were said to have been the police.

One of the most noticeably absent luxuries at Mustafa Khalid bin Rachman was privacy. Phone calls home to Australia were not only extremely difficult to make but any received had to be taken in the nursing office and were considered public property. Everyone listened unashamedly and made comments. As for mail, there was the usual pillaging, looting and losing of our precious letters and parcels by the postal pixies.

The deputy chief nurse, Sister Immaculata, was a very gentle and sweet Filipina. I was horrified to hear that for the two years she had been working at Mustafa KBR the switchboard operator had phoned her every hour, all night long.

'Whatever for?' I asked.

She shrugged. 'I am the only Filipina who has a phone and a room to herself. I suppose it is to check that I am there and behaving myself.'

After about a month I had finally achieved my major objective. The hospital was clean, all three floors of it, and life was not too bad. There was a more congenial working atmosphere than at KFH, but I still had no desire to stay.

4 The long way home

At the end of six weeks I still hadn't seen the colour of the company's money, not even my current wages. Pay day had come and gone for everyone else, but not me, though I did have a guarantee that it was on the way. The company was extra keen to keep me now, because the hospital director insisted that he wanted me to stay. I was biding my time to give them notice as soon as my money was in my hot little hand, because I knew well how little a promise meant to this collection of crooks. They thought that promises were like pie-crust, made to be broken.

Life crawled on, its tedium of hard work and long hours broken only by traumas and farces. I was hauled before the hospital director to answer someone's serious complaint about the morality of the place. The little hospital nighties in the children's ward, oh, horror, sported images of teenagers dancing rock and roll! No, I did not make them, buy them or have anything else to do with them, but I was in charge of the nursing service, and the nurses put them on the children, so naturally I was to blame. There was an amazing to do about this. In the end I got off with a written reprimand, on condition that I apologise to the outraged parent and put the offending nighties in the incinerator. And we were so short of linen!

Not long afterwards the hospital director called for me again. This time the complaint involved a farewell party held by the nurses, female only of course. I wasn't at it and I did not know about it, but said that I had given permission. It was easier all round; they couldn't do too much to me. I received another warning letter. These warning letters were meant to have you quaking in your boots. One copy went to the offender, one copy went on file, one went to the salary officer, and one to the hospital director. The Ministry of Health usually then deducted from one to five days of the criminal's pay. They could not do this to me, however, as they couldn't get their hands on my pay (neither could I, for that matter) because I was paid by the company. One nurse lost five days pay for sleeping in and being late for night duty. If you got more than three warnings you could be charged with insubordination and deported.

Jubilation! After ten weeks as an unpaid slave I finally received some money. Not quite all the back pay I was owed, but enough to feel that I had won my point and could retire gracefully. I put in my resignation. It boomeranged. A brief note, scribbled across my letter by the head of the company in Riyadh, said that it was not accepted. Maybe this was going to be harder than I thought.

A short time before Christmas, the Egyptian manager of the Sheraton hotel, who was grateful because I had been kind to his elderly uncle when he was a patient, invited me to bring some friends to a free lunch at the hotel on one of our Fridays off. I recruited some of the company staff and we chose to go on the Friday before Christmas day. We managed, after a lot of dithering, to get written permission from the company administrator and the hospital director. The females went in the company bus, but the men had to walk the two kilometres.

Otherwise, it might have looked as though we were going partying. All participating infidels were finally mustered at the hotel. The Sheraton's manager, being of a liberal bent, put up some decorations before we arrived, but the religious police came and made him take them down. We said to him, 'Don't worry. Its not Christmas we are celebrating, but someone's birthday.'

I tried again to tender my resignation. It came back again, but this time with a letter offering me the post of director of nursing at King Abdul Aziz hospital in Riyadh. I refused, but was flattered. They had offered me the best they had.

I heard from my spies in KFH that Sister Fatma, the fearsome assistant chief nurse, had been sacked and thrown out of the country because her husband had been accused of being a Palestinian terrorist. He had apparently been involved in some guerilla warfare in his spare time when they were home on leave in Palestine: the Saudis do not take kindly to this sort of thing. Fatma was also said to have forged the qualifications that got her husband his job as a nurse in a small clinic outside Medina. It would surprise me to find a nurse in those clinics with a genuine set of papers. Fatma and co. were given no warning, and had to leave instantly. I only saw the husband once, but he looked a meek little fellow. She had more the build for terrorism. If she fell in wet concrete they could have used the mould to make Mack trucks. One black look from her always threw me into a cold sweat.

I tendered my resignation for the third time and it was refused again. I began to worry that they really were not going to let me go. I told the company directors I was going to take my case to the Labour Court which settled these grievances, and also ask for my money. They laughed. Did I not know that the Labour Court was inside Medina where I, under pain of death, could not go? They also said they would not pay me any more unless I agreed to stay. So another pay day came and went without salary for me.

Once again it was a Saudi who came to my rescue. One of the MOH department directors, who had heard of my problem, offered to take a letter of complaint to the court for me. None of the Muslims in the company could do so without reprisals, so I would not ask them. A representative of the court phoned me on receipt of my letter, listened to my story and said he would start an official investigation.

Two young English females arrived about this time. They had been employed by the company as secretaries. When I first saw them I thought they were sisters. They could have been clones. Both had pale blonde hair in dreary wash-and-wear perms. They wore the same style of clothes and identical, coloured plastic hair clips. Both were the same height and size, about twelve kilos overweight (considered perfection in Saudi). It could be seen on closer inspection that one was slightly prettier than the other. Not long after they arrived we went on one of our trips to Jeddah. The prettier of the two bouncy blondes put on tons of make-up, lots of electric-blue eye-shadow, and let a lock of fair hair escape from the front of her scarf. The local men in the market were riveted by her. I encountered her in an electrical shop where the assistant was showing her a radio. He never took his eyes from her face. His hands had a life of their own, demonstrating and doing their thing with the radio. His offsider stood by, mouth agape, eyes cemented to her, positively drooling, while I was utterly ignored.

As we drove the six hours back to Medina through the soft grey gloom of twilight in the desert, the two blondes slept off an excess of admiration, lying on the back seat across Sister Olive, the overstuffed sofa. She made a good pillow – which was fortunate, as she was not much use for anything else.

At long last the Labour Court told Omega they had to pay up and let me leave. I had been packed and ready for weeks, and needed only to wait a few days for my exit visa. Things were bad at this time in the Arabian Gulf. Kuwait had been attacked, and another attempt had been made to land on the eastern coast of Saudi Arabia. I was glad I'd decided to travel in the opposite direction, taking the long way home via Egypt.

I have a passion for ships, boats and sea travel, so I had studied the map to see if it would be possible to return to Australia this way, instead of by plane. I knew there was a ship that went regularly from Jeddah in Saudi to Suez in Egypt, and it appeared likely that another ship could be found there to travel down the coast of Africa to southern Egypt, from where I could make my way into Sudan. The Sudanese I had worked with in Saudi had all been such friendly, kind people that I wanted to see their country. It was written of in the travel books as one of the world's last frontiers, much of it still unexplored, a destination for 'only the hardiest and most adventurous travellers'. Sudanese friends told me I would be able to travel there alone despite it being under *sharia* – governed by the holy laws of Islam – and that I could negotiate my way to Sudan from Egypt by river boat and train. If no boats were available I would travel overland. It would probably take several months, but that did not bother me.

I asked Faoud, the young Ethiopian who handled travel arrangements for the company, about taking a boat across the Red Sea to Egypt. He looked shocked, 'Nobody goes that way,' he said.

'Is there any law that says I can't?' I asked, explaining to him that I wanted to go 'the long way home'.

He said it was permitted, but not advisable. 'It is not for you.'

'What do you mean? Other people must go that way.'

'You are different.'

How well I knew this! 'Is it because I am a non-believer? ' I asked.

'Well' – he hesitated, seeking the right words so as not to offend me – 'mostly they are pilgrims. Simple people.'

(Simple! How simple was I? I would not have been in Saudi at all had my faculties been giant ones. And I had returned! 'Retarded' was more the word for it.)

'Would I offend them?'

His eyes moved to my tightly-wound white head covering. 'No, mostly not.'

'Then I shall go!'

I made a booking to leave Jeddah for Suez by ship on 18 January, through Faoud but still against his protestations.

There seems to exist a Murphy's-type law that decrees that whenever you arrange to travel by a certain means of transport, you hear news of manifold disasters involving these same conveyances. In the next few days ships went down with all hands all over the place. The ferry to Rangoon (which I once travelled on) sank; three hundred people were drowned. The boat which plies the crossing between Java and Sumatra sank with one hundred lives. A ship sank in the Red Sea out of Mogadishu, exactly where I hoped to be boating soon. A coastal steamer caught fire off the African coast and everyone on it died.

I had even more misgivings when I received my ship's ticket and read the rules. First and foremost, in large print, was the warning that passengers were not to light cooking fires on the deck. It was a worry but, considering the planes that had been falling out of the air – three Burma Air and a Garuda had bit the dust in the last year – and the buses that had been crashing all over Egypt, the alternatives did not look much better. Rebels and border warriors all stepped up operations dramatically in the areas I intended to go, adding interest to my proposed venture. To top it off, the volcano I climbed in Sumatra erupted and killed a couple of people. I wondered if this was an omen. I supposed I could try a camel caravan.

5 Passage to Egypt

Abdul Aizzat, the lecherous company administrator, trying even to the last to fondle my knee, drove me to the airport to catch the plane to Jeddah and presented me with a bottle of my favourite perfume, *Femme*, and an expensive-looking pen with which to continue our alleged friendship by post. It was useless to protest, so I accepted with grace. I did not want to cause any complications at this stage.

I spent two nights in Jeddah at the Kaki hotel, organising my departure. I had a last look at the old town and visited the Beduin *souk* – the original bazaar of Jeddah, where it is still possible to buy, but not cheaply, the old guns and armaments so beloved of the Arab, lovely old weapons forged by skilled craftsmen for the warriors of Islam, who used them to kill in the name of Allah.

The company representative in Jeddah, a Lebanese called Ashard, had been given the job of ferrying me around, always accompanied by a suitable chaperon. It was his responsibility to see that I actually left and did not slip away to stay on illegally. (Perish the thought! I was only too willing to shake the sand of Saudi Arabia from my shoes.) Being taken care of was one of the few perks of being a helpless female, and I did not mind at all. I was chauffeured around as though I was an invalid or a mentally defective four-year-old.

Ashard helped me to arrange the air freight home of some of my baggage so that I could set off with less encumbrance. I refrain from saying 'travel light', as this is something I can never do, although I dearly wish I could. I had an enormous suitcase (The Monster), a large overnight bag, a well stuffed handbag and an umbrella as travelling companions.

I phoned home to notify the family of my movements. I was still apprehensive. Even though I had got this far, I did not feel I could breathe easily until I was actually out of Saudi. I could still be stopped from leaving, and felt the company might be vindictive enough to find some reason to do so.

Finally the eighteenth, Oh! happy day, arrived. The ship was sailing at five in the evening. Ashard and chaperon arrived at two, and we drove to the wharf, about an hour away. For two thousand years the area around the wharf had been the heart and life blood of Jeddah and it was still a busy place. My ship was tied up at a dock in the centre of a large enclosed area. To reach it I needed first to go through customs and the immigration shed. Ashard saw me through customs and, at the immigration counter, when I stepped over the line marking the end of Saudi jurisdiction – had reached the point of no return and was safely on my way out – I was able to lean back and take my passport from him. Fantastic. I had almost made it. But I was still sweating.

Outside the shed I found myself in the open and there, in the distance, I could see the *Al Lhara* alongside the wharf. I joined a large crowd of intending passengers, who all looked to be Egyptian or Sudanese. Many of them were pilgrims, for ferrying the Guests of God was the ship's principal business. I shoved my suitcase along in front of me as we inched towards her. It was hot in the sun, so I dropped my long black head scarf down over my face and retired into oblivion behind the veil. Some of the men pushed my bag to the head of the line. This is another of the perks for females in Muslim countries such as Saudi and Egypt. Women are not expected to stand in line behind men – it is not seemly.

After an hour or so, I made it up the gangplank, and a very surprised officer in a smart white uniform escorted me to my cabin. I was a rare animal in that neck of the woods. Most of the passengers were travelling deck class and none of them were westerners.

I went out on deck to watch the ship depart. Although I now had the waters of the Red Sea beneath my feet, I still could not feel free until I had seen the last of the shore disappear. The Egyptian purser invited me on to the bridge to watch from there. I met the captain, a beefy, hairy fellow, but a very jolly one. To my surprise he used English-language terms, bellowing, 'Full ahead,' and 'Steady as she goes,' down the speaking tube as he gave orders for our departure. I had thought these were only used in Hollywood films.

The anchor came up slowly and we began to edge away from the wharf and glide along the breakwater, which was made of dun-coloured concrete and jutted a long way out to sea. On the end of it was one of the hideous pieces of concrete sculpture the Saudis are so fond of. It rose thirty metres or so in the air and resembled a set of elongated fingers reaching skyward.

We sailed dead on the dot of five and, as if that feat were not astounding enough for an Egyptian ship, meals were on time too.

Jeddah was not attractive from the sea. There was none of the charming old town to be seen. It was all black smoke streaming from rows of industrial buildings and the usual ugly port-side line up of wharves, silos, cranes and oil tanks. But there were many ships from different nations anchored at the wharves and in the harbour. Not a breath of wind disturbed the surface of the sea which lay flat, calm and blue under the cloudless sky. I stood watching the breakwater and the shore, barren, beige and colourless, gradually becoming smaller and smaller, and was terribly glad when I saw the last of Saudi Arabia slip away beneath the horizon. All its hassles, troubles, restrictions and complications were receding from me, *Al hum del'lah* – Praise be to Allah, Most Merciful, Most Compassionate.

Bouncing along euphorically, filled with the joy of living, I made my way below deck to investigate the possibilities offered by this floating rescuer of maidens in distress.

The *Al Lhara* was the best ship on the Saudi–Egypt run: although a mere child of eight years, she looked more like an old lady of eighty. She was tatty and careworn. I was assured by one of the crew that she was about to be painted next week. (Isn't everything?) The Middle Eastern cure-all is paint. Tart it up with a thick coat of paint, make it look better and this will reverse its disrepair and make it run better too. I remained sceptical about next week's paint job. It sounded like just another *bukra en shal'lah* – tomorrow, God willing.

I have heard recently that the *Al Lhara* sank on one of her regular runs across the Red Sea and most of the passengers perished.

My cabin was on the top deck. It was small and grotty. There were torn pillowcases and linen on the bunk and the toilet was booby-trapped – every time I went near it some part fell on the floor.

The dining room was surprising – it was spotless. The starched white tablecloths were covered by clear plastic that was thumb-tacked to the wooden edges of the tables. This was a wise precaution in view of the manners of the locals at table. The room was adorned by large vases of gruesome imitation plastic flowers. The lighting was fluorescent and the whole atmosphere reminiscent of an old fashioned café in Kalgoorlie. But the table service was utterly silver spoon. I wondered if this was a relic that had survived from British colonial days. The waiters, like the rest of the crew, apart from the Egyptian officers, were mostly Sudanese or Nubian. The food was another surprise. It was excellent, the only flaw being dessert – generally a great slab of luridly coloured jelly sitting wobbling, naked and obscene, in the middle of a big, flat, white plate. The drinks were tea, coffee or Pepsi, the *Al Lhara* was a 'dry' ship.

I had been told that I could change money on the ship but this turned out to be another Saudi fairy story. The ship took only Egyptian, Saudi or American cash. I had only a few remaining Riyals and four American dollars, but I managed. The food was very cheap and there was no bar or shop on this ship to tempt me. I always travel with a few dollar notes for emergencies, as I have yet to find a place in all the world where they cannot be used when all else fails.

I enjoyed the voyage, though the sea was sometimes very rough. Luckily I am a good sailor and am never seasick. One day I watched a magnificent *dhow*, the wooden Arab sailing ship whose style has remained unchanged for thousands of years because it is perfection, pass close by our bows. Her name was *El Habib*, the beloved, and she well deserved it, winging her way along under the press of full, billowing canvas.

At half past eight on the third morning, the ship arrived at Port Tewfik, which is on the southern entrance to the Suez canal and three kilometres from the town of Suez. I made ready to leave, but it was two hours before I was called to the immigration line-up. I did not disembark until noon.

I had been told that it was unnecessary for an Australian to have a visa before arriving in Egypt, because one could be obtained on entry. This was true, but it was a huge hassle. The large tin edifices housing the official functionaries were packed to the brim, and were sweaty places to spend long hours in. I was still wearing my *abeya* and head covering, partly out of habit and partly because I felt it was probably better to do so – this part of Egypt was not much accustomed to western women. I was nearly expiring underneath my wraps by the time I'd finished my slow progress through customs and immigration. First I'd had to walk a country mile to the other end of the wharf enclosure to get a visa. Then I'd had to track back to the point I had started from to change money at the bank to pay for the visa. Then I had to return all the way back to collect it. At last, however, I was through the arrival formalities, and was deposited in Suez on the doorstep of a waterside hostelry by an obliging taxi driver whom I had asked to take me 'somewhere suitable'.

6 Ships in the night

The hotel was called the Summer Palace. It didn't live up to its name, but was comfortable enough and reasonably cheap. The staff were obliging and, as a sign in fractured English on the front counter informed me, 'dilated to serve'. Someone had attempted to make gardens and, although they weren't lush, they were welcome after the barrenness of Saudi. I had a room on the second floor, looking down on the gardens and over the bay.

The hotel had a restaurant set apart in its grounds and I made a bee-line there for sustenance. I was not disappointed. The food was good, cheap and plentiful, consisting mostly of fresh, locally-caught fish. There was a bar at the entrance to the restaurant so I indulged in a couple of drinks to celebrate my freedom. Then I partook of an enormous lunch of several courses, served in the garden where tables and chairs stood under the shade of bright canvas umbrellas. When the bill was presented and I found the total cost of this sumptuous decadence amounted to just six Egyptian pounds, or around four dollars, my day was made.

I spent the next five days resting in that quietly beautiful place, rejoicing in being free again and consuming leisurely meals in the restaurant, a cross between a shade house and a pergola, where sparrows and other birds had taken up residence and paid for their lodging by cleaning the floor of crumbs and scraps, hopping happily between the diners' feet.

From the balcony outside my bedroom, or even from my bed, I could watch ships on the broad expanse of the harbour: big ships, always at least thirty of them, moving in or out or riding at anchor; fishing boats with colourful sails; and a motley collection of tough little work-horses. At night, against the black velvet sky, their lights bobbed and flickered like fireflies.

After a couple of forays to Suez in taxis I learned how to use the communal transport vehicles, rather like the *bemos* of Indonesia – small vans into which the attendant squeezes as many passengers as will fit without too much complaining. You had only to stand anywhere by the side of the road, wave an arm in the air, and one would screech to a halt at your feet, take your ten-cent fare and cram you in.

I saw everywhere the scars and ravages left by the wars of 1967 and 1973 with Israel, in which Suez had been almost totally destroyed. There were many bombed-out remnants of buildings, often housing squatters, with walls riddled with bullet and shell holes. Rubble littered the streets, but rebuilding was going on.

There are few tourist attractions in Suez apart from the ships passing in and out of the Canal. But it is one of the main departure points for the *Haj* to Saudi Arabia, and I saw here, as throughout the rest of Egypt, signs painted on the house walls of those who had made the pilgrimage to Mecca and could now call themselves *Hadji*. These pictures were often in the form of a colourful, if naive, painting of their means of travel: a bus, plane or car. Modern hieroglyphics – most of the people cannot read.

Suez is over-crowded, scruffy and much of it is dirty, but it is exotic. The buildings were square, several storeys high and coloured white through to brown. Most roofs were flat, but occasionally there rose a red-tiled, pitched and gabled one. Here and there among the buildings a palm tree or minaret raised its head. Along the water's edge jostled battered fishing vessels, expensive pleasure craft and yachts. The old town had one main street of small shops, and a few more shops in some of the little streets that ran off it. Here there were *souks* catering only for the locals – no tourist trash to be found. From jovial, rotund men in well-worn caftans I bought raisins, bananas, coconut and sesame seeds from hessian bags open on the ground, and handfuls of costume jewellery, lots of fun and super cheap. Hair ornaments were also very popular and, not wanting to be out of fashion, I bought some butterflies to pin up my hair.

There were a few restaurants in the main street, but they were obviously not accustomed to western tourists. (In the time I spent in Suez the only westerners I saw were a pair of French businessmen.) One menu, however, had made an attempt at English sub-titles, and offered the dubious delicacy of 'mushroom soap'. I had a meal in another restaurant and asked to be shown to the 'Ladies'. This restaurant was a very classy joint; it had an inside rest room. I did not realise just how 'inside' until the waiter led me to it. It was right there in the dining room! Its door, which had a two foot gap between where it finished and the floor, opened directly off the side wall. By then it was too late to refuse and not look a fool, so I had to make do with a squat toilet, a mere hole in the tiled floor, practically in the packed dining room, from where my feet, and heaven knows what else, were clearly visible to the lucky people outside. I felt as though

I was giving the after-dinner entertainment and an unpaid performance at that.

My first port of call on my initial visit to the town was the post office, where I sent telegrams to my family and friends, then postcards to everyone else I knew, declaring my liberation. It was very cheap to develop film in Egypt, so I had all the films processed that I had been saving from Saudi. I hadn't wanted to risk their mutilation by the censor. One British nurse had had her photo taken with her favourite uncle before she left home. He died shortly afterwards but her last photo of him, and its negative, were destroyed when she sent the film for developing in Saudi, because she was holding his hand.

Having decided to try travelling down the Egyptian coast to Aswan, or anywhere else possible, by sea, I went looking for a ship and spent a lot of time sitting about in the offices of various shipping agents. Although I met some friendly souls, I eventually gave up. They all thought I was queer because I did not want to fly like every other tourist, and did not comprehend when I tried to explain about wanting to take the long way home. They were probably right.

I was adopted during my search by a well-fed, fatherly shipping agent, who drove me around the maritime companies to try my luck. I learned from them that the days of passenger sea travel have almost gone. The big ships now only pass through Suez and do not stop there. I realised that I would have to take a bus to Cairo and try to find a river steamer down to Aswan instead.

My friend took me on a tour of the sights. The canal amazed me. It looked as though it had just been dug. I had always imagined it to be enormous, but it seemed only a matter of metres across. When a large ship passes through the canal it literally fills the narrow crevice, seeming almost to touch the sides as it towers over them. To see thirty or more big ships and tankers moving majestically in stately procession up the canal was a thrilling sight for a ship lover like me. I longed to be travelling on one of them.

The shipping agent told me that there has been a canal linking the Red Sea and the Mediterranean since ancient times. The modern canal was completed in 1869, at a cost of millions of pounds and the lives of thousands of workers. Much of the money involved was spent on lavish celebrations, including a four-day party and a grand ball, to impress the guests at the opening. After the massive spend-up Pasha Ismail, the Egyptian ruler, was left so deficient in funds that he had to sell half his share of the canal to the British government and a period of British control in Egypt followed.

After I had rested and restored my soul, I bought a bus ticket to Cairo on the vehicle advertised as 'deluxe'. I had seen the 'regular' buses broken down in droves by the roadside on my previous trip to Egypt, and been warned off them. The ticket cost the princely sum of one dollar fifty and included a lunch box, which was not at all princely. A boiled egg and a dry bun rattled around forlornly in a big cardboard container. Buses in this country are only for tourists with iron nerves and stomachs of steel. It took us two hours to cover the 135 kilometres to Cairo, passing all the way the skeletons of vehicles gone to that great garage in the sky. The narrow road was often blocked by donkey carts and camel drays, which held up the traffic until the bus driver, casting caution to the wind, roared out to pass them, displaying total disregard for the lives of his passengers. I sat tensely, my foot stamping on the brake for him. The locals remained blissfully unconcerned, secure in the knowledge, perhaps, that Allah, the All Merciful, held them in the palm of His hand.

On arrival in Cairo, I dropped my shaky remains into a taxi, went straight to Shepheard's hotel, and sought solace at the bar.

7 Shepheard's delight

Shepheard's is a famous old hotel in the style of Raffles of Singapore. It reposes on the bank of the River Nile, in the Midan Tahir district, which is roughly the centre of Cairo. Shepheard's was the place where the famous and notorious stayed in the past – royalty, adventurers, intriguers and spies. It was burned down during riots in 1952, but rebuilt in the same style. It has character and old world charm and still scores four tourist guide book stars. I took a single room, after bargaining for my worker's discount. Produce a Middle Eastern work permit, and the price usually drops thirty to fifty per cent.

It took three porters to escort me, with many flourishes, into the original old wood-panelled lift that had been salvaged from the first hotel. It trundled, protesting all the way with creaks and groans, to the fourth floor, where I was shown to a room and divested of my small cash.

The rooms of the hotel were large, had balconies overlooking the Nile, much dark, vintage furniture, and a profusion of brass lamps and fittings. Even the waste basket was brass. I especially liked what I called the walk-in mirror. For an unfathomable reason my room had a tiny, three-sided alcove with floor-to-ceiling mirrors. There was just enough space to walk in and admire yourself, but its real purpose eluded me. There was a terrific view of the river from the large plate-glass doors which ran the full length of the room and opened on a balcony four floors above the Nile.

On arrival in Egypt all foreigners, except South Africans and Taiwanese, who are prohibited entry, must report to the police within twenty-four hours to register their persons. When I went down to hotel reception on my first morning in Cairo, I found that the staff had already accomplished this feat for me. I was relieved. It can be a lengthy ordeal to make any arrangements in Egypt. Even buying a ticket on a train or bus can involve hours of hard work. Visitors are advised to come complete with infinite patience.

Because of its size exploring Cairo wasn't easy. Egyptians call their capital *Misr Egypt* – mother of the world – and they're not wrong. It is made up of many districts including Medieval Cairo, the City of the Dead, the Citadel of Antiquity, Old Cairo and Coptic Cairo. Numerous bridges cross the Nile to connect the various districts and the two islands, Gezira and Rhoda, in between. To reach most areas I had to find some kind of transport, and even that was not always easy. Hailing a taxi at peak hours took lots of staying power. The accepted method is to stand at the side of the road, waving an arm vigorously, screaming your destination. When you do get one, the local custom is to share. People piled in on top of me, smiling and friendly, put their sticky brats on my knees, and proceeded to investigate my shopping. At least this took my eyes off the road, where innumerable folk seemed about to commit suicide under our wheels.

I did not even attempt to travel on a bus. I am simply not that rugged and the sight of them was enough for me. They are packed until almost bursting at the seams, their windows and doors having been removed to make room for still more passengers. People hang all over the outsides like burrs on a sheep.

I set out from Shepheard's to explore the surrounding Midan Tahir district on foot: not as dangerous an occupation as it is in some areas of Cairo, which is the largest city in Africa and teems with people. Midan Tahir has overhead walkways across the worst of the traffic for those not bent on self-destruction. This is the main tourist territory of Cairo, containing the magnificent Egyptian Museum and western-type hotels and shops.

I made my way, bumped and jostled by the throngs on the streets, to the Kasr el Nil, which is one of Cairo's two westernised shopping streets and crammed with attractive items at reasonable prices, as well as flashy goods designed to tempt the tourist. I especially liked the pill box hat, scarf and veil sets that are part of smart Egyptian women's outfits, and couldn't resist one that was made of beige silk and embroidered with countless tiny seed pearls. Halfway down the Kasr el Nil I came across a little shop with the uninviting name of Poo-Pee. In the window reposed an elegant nightie and dressing gown which were, the sign declared boldly, a 'negligent set of under cloths'. Well, they should know!

I stopped for lunch at the famous old Estoril restaurant, which stands just off the Kasr el Nil. Egyptian food is nothing to rave about, but it's edible. I demolished large quantities of *ta'amiyya*, little balls of fried chick peas and spices, and *kufta*, minced spiced meat balls cooked like kebabs on a stick. Later I sat outside under an awning drinking *shai* – tea, which is served poisonously full of sugar, in diminutive, glass-handled mugs – and watched the endless stream of people. The men strolled by in western clothes or the *galabaya* caftan, *hadji* cap or white turban adorning their heads. Some women wore *abeyas* and were veiled, but many wore western-style ankle-length skirts. Very few Egyptian women show any leg.

Although many Egyptian women are now unveiled, few enjoy western freedom. Men see protection of their female family members as their duty. I heard foreign women complain that they were bothered by unwelcome attentions from Egyptian men, but often their dress or behaviour was inappropriate. A woman must look 'respectable' (in Muslim eyes) to be treated with respect in this country. Anyway, the harassment is usually only verbal. Men say to you, 'Hello, I love you,' and, 'You are beautiful.' I found this easy to ignore. There are, after all, a lot worse things you can hear. 'You are ugly,' for a start.

Everywhere I went I was accosted by beggars. They are a sad fact of life in Cairo. My only solution was to keep a pocketful of small change and give this away. The stories I heard about begging being a great racket, and that they all have Rolls Royces parked around the corner and therefore should be ignored, do not wash with me.

It was winter in Cairo and the weather was warm by day and cool at night and, as it rarely rained, the sky was usually a bright blue. But the *khamseen* had been blowing for a few days. This is the horrible hot wind that churns up sandstorms in the desert and sends them swirling through the streets of Cairo, turning the sky beige, obliterating the sun and making the river the *eau de Nil* colour described by couturiers. On these days I returned from every trip out with my clothes and face filthy, my hair standing stiff on end with dirt and desert sand crunching between my teeth. No wonder I made straight for the bar and some liquid refreshment to wash the grit away.

Although Egypt is a Muslim country, alcohol is freely available in hotels and restaurants, but can only be bought, albeit quite cheaply, from a few scattered wine shops. On the streets and in the squares hawkers sold luscious, luridly-coloured drinks such as *saleb*, made from milk, rice flour, grapes and coconut. I tried it in cafés but resisted the urge on the street, knowing that the combination of ice and milk in doubtful conditions made instant typhoid a strong possibility.

One morning I went to the Khan el Khalili, a six-hundred-year-old bazaar, reputedly the biggest in the Middle East, located in the Islamic district of Cairo. The taxi dropped me in a drab street full of small shops, some with lairy tourist junk hanging from their front awnings. At first I thought I was in the wrong place, but on closer inspection I discovered that there were narrow alleys, accessible only to pedestrians and donkeys, leading in from between one or two of the shops. Elbowing my way in, I was suddenly in the fabled bazaar itself – a stupendous Alladin's cave!

The Khan el Khalili began as a *caravanserai*, a place for caravans to stop and rest. Built in 1382 AD by Garkas el Khalili, the Master of the Horse of the Sultan Barquq, it evolved over centuries into a market where traders, dealers and buyers from all over the world met to bargain and barter. It is a huge conglomeration of tiny shops, *souks* and workshops where craftsmen work – using archaic tools identical to those drawn on the walls of the pharaohs' tombs – and sell their wares: inlaid boxes, leather work, brass and copper items, carvings, wood work, paintings on papyrus, and pottery. Gold and silver are sold by weight, at a price set every day according to the price of bullion.

I wandered up and down in this fabulous place for hours, through minute alleys and mazes of stalls, stopping now and then to look at costume jewellery, perfume, fabrics, flowers, fruit, vegetables and an exotic range of spices – cinnamon, saffron, cloves and ginger. There were masses of antiquities, but I resisted buying, knowing that they were mainly of the 'made yesterday' variety. Often the copies are very good – some even have the seal of approval (also copied) of the Director of Antiquities from the Egyptian Museum. It is a case of *caveat emptor* – buyer beware!

Despite the density of goods and humanity, the pace was relaxed and the traders did not hassle me. Some tried to lure me into their shops with offers of wondrous bargains, such as a 'chromium plaited bowel', but didn't mind when I declined.

I stopped for some mint tea and a rest at a bantam-sized café, and sat there blissfully while all around me the trading went on as it had done for centuries.

From the steps in front of Shepheard's I took a water-bus, one of the many which cross the Nile in all directions for a few cents a ride. The instant I stepped ashore across the river in the district of Old Cairo, I was transported back seven hundred years. Antiquated wooden houses, several storeys high were jammed shoulder-to-shoulder along the narrow streets, and now and then extraordinary old palaces appeared, hung with carved wooden balconies. Map in hand, I negotiated my way through the narrow streets and squares packed with people. Women in *purdah* gossiped from upper windows or lowered baskets on ropes so the egg man or fish man could send up their wares. Men sat at tables on the pavement in front of small cafés, playing dominoes or chess. I dodged donkeys, camels and goats, and manoeuvred my way to the Al Rifa'i Mosque where many Muslim Arab royal personages have found their eternal resting places. I saw the tomb of the Shah of Iran and the tomb of King Farouk of Egypt – he of the infamous excesses, whose appetite for the good things of life was probably the reason he landed here somewhat prematurely. He made a full-time occupation of extravagant spending, chasing women and eating. One of his snacks could have fed half the third world's starving poor. He apparently consumed five chickens at a sitting, and that was just for starters. I have a great interest in food, but think that is going a bit far.

Near here I also found the mausoleum of Shagarat al Durr, built in 1250 AD. I liked the gruesome story of this very liberated lady.

Shagarat al Durr was the only female Muslim ruler in history. She was taken as a slave from a nomadic tribe and married to the last head of the Ayyubid dynasty at a time when Cairo was under attack from the Crusaders. Her husband died, but she pretended he was still alive, and ruled for three months through his supposed orders until her son returned from abroad to take over. The son, however, proved to be a dead loss at the ruling business, so she had him killed and announced herself Sultana of Egypt. She ruled for eighty days, but the Abbasid caliph of Baghdad refused to accept her position, so she married the leader of the Marmelukes, and ruled through him. All went well until he foolishly took another wife. This peeved Shagarat enormously, so she had him killed and threw the wife in prison. The Marmelukes discovered this, cast *her* in prison and let the second wife out. The latter, naturally, was a little aggrieved and, not being the type to forgive and forget, she and her ladies took Shagarat, beat her to death with wooden bats and hung her body out over the citadel's walls as dog food (the forerunner of Pal?). In time someone salvaged the remains and put them away in this tomb.

The moral of this story is that it's better to be one wife among many, than no wife of any.

In my hotel I read up on history, and learned that the ancient Egyptians possibly evolved from a mixture of local stone-age people and immigrants from the Libyan desert, Central Africa and Arabia.

By 3000 BC Egypt had become a powerful nation, building magnificent temples and pyramids. Eventually Egypt's lucky star waned and a long history of invasions began. Everyone had a turn. Libya, Ethiopia, Persia, Assyria, the Greeks – Alexander the Great built his absolutely fabulous city of Alexandria on the coast – and the Romans. They gave protection to several rulers, one of whom was Cleopatra the seventh, heroine of stage and film ever since. Roman general Mark Antony came, saw and conquered Cleopatra and they lived happily together for ten years, which provoked the ire of the powers in Rome. Octavian was sent to chastise them. Antony and Cleopatra lost the deciding battle and, in a fit of pique, committed suicide. But they are still together; their embalmed bodies rest side by side in a tomb beneath the soil of Alexandria. I had visited them on my first journey to the Middle East.

After the fall of the Roman empire the Arabs conquered Egypt and spread Islam, and when they, in their turn, were evicted, more conquerors came and went. Salah al Din, who defeated the Christian crusaders, lasted until ousted by the Turks in 1517. Napoleon arrived in 1798 but stayed only a month before the British admiral, Lord Nelson, defeated him in a naval battle off the coast of Alexandria. The British appointed a viceroy to rule Egypt under their guidance until 1922 when Egypt became independent under King Fuad I. During World War Two Egypt again came under British protection, which lasted until 1952, when Colonel Gamel Nasser overthrew King Farouk, the son of King Fuad, and formed an Islamic republic.

During my stay, I was surprised to find that, although Egypt is a Muslim country, there is much tolerance for other religions. In Old Cairo there are sites that are places of pilgrimage for Jews, Christians and Muslims alike. I visited the Jewish synagogue where legend says the prophet Jeremiah is buried, and the spring that marks the place where Moses was supposed to have been found in the bullrushes, and where Mary washed the baby Jesus after the holy family's flight to Egypt to escape the wrath of Herod.

Christianity was brought to Egypt, one of the first countries to embrace it, by Saint Mark in 61 AD. He landed at Alexandria and began preaching and baptising. Seven years later he was martyred in the street by an angry mob consisting of fans of the Greek-Egyptian god, Serapis. Despite this, Christian numbers grew steadily and in Roman times, when persecution of Christians was the national sport, 800,000 Christians migrated here. Coptic (the word copt means Egypt) Christianity became the state religion for five hundred years. Copts now comprise only about thirteen per cent of the population, but because they have not intermarried they have retained the physical features of ancient Egypt, the narrow elegant faces with long slanting eyes straight from the walls of five-thousand-year-old tombs.

I allocated one of my days in Cairo entirely to the Egyptian Museum, which contains over 100,000 antiquities from all eras of Egypt's history. The most famous rooms are the ones containing the furnishings found in the tomb of Tutankhamun. This was the only pharaoh's tomb ever found intact; the seals on the door were still unbroken when the tomb was found. Although Tutankhamun was an unimportant king, who died at the age of eighteen, having ruled only nine years, his tomb contained fabulous wealth. After three thousand years the king's mummified body was discovered exactly as it had been left. Three coffins had been placed over it in succession, two of gilded wood and one of solid gold, as well as the fabulous mask of gold, lapis lazuli and gems that was put over the inner coffin. Then they were all placed in a big stone sarcophagus. This remains in a tomb at Luxor with the outer coffin while the other 1700 treasures – there were three chambers of chariots, weapons, food, clothes, a stupendous amount of gold (more than two hundred kilograms) and jewels – are displayed in twelve rooms here. I wonder what the loot from the tomb of Rameses III, who ruled for sixty-five years, would have been.

I ventured further south the next day, this time to see Imbaba, the *Souk el Gahmell*; the biggest camel market in the country. The taxi stopped among masses of modern houses and, once again, I thought I was in the wrong place. I walked to the end of the street and suddenly the market materialised, looking totally out of place in this modern suburb, as if conjured up by the genie's magic spell. In an unpaved square from which arose a cacophony of sound and movement, shrouded in a cloud of dust stirred up by their milling feet, I found a horde of men and camels. For centuries caravans of camels have been herded up the Forty Days' Road from Sudan to Aswan, then brought here to Imbaba. Today a good one sells for around twelve hundred Australian dollars.

Deciding a camel would be too hard, even for me, to smuggle through customs, I withdrew from the sale and found a café. I sat down to study my map, and saw that further south again from here was the district of Giza, which extended to the edge of the desert where the pyramids were. I decided it was time I went to see them.

8 My Frouzi friend

Suddenly they appeared by the side of the road in the empty desert. The pyramids: symbol of Egypt throughout the world. They stood alone, the same colour as the sand from which they seemed to have sprung, against an intense blue sky.

I had travelled to Giza by tourist bus; an eleven-kilometre journey that had taken an hour to cover, so heavy was the traffic. This road had been paved to honour the visit of America's President Jimmy Carter. (More power to him, it must have been quite a ride before.) At last, I was standing in awe before the wonders of the world.

Here, at Giza, there are three main pyramids and the Sphinx, an impressive 4500 years old. In the vicinity are lesser pyramids of the wives of pharaohs, and the *mastabas* and tombs of princes and nobles. The three major pyramids are the Great Pyramid of Cheops; the pyramid of Chephren, his son; and that of Mycerinus, Cheops's grandson. They are all built of local stone from the Moqattam hills. Cheops, the greatest, oldest, and largest pyramid, stands 147 metres high, took 2,500,000 limestone blocks, each weighing two and a half tonnes, twenty years, and 100,000 slaves, to build. Each year a few folk fall to their deaths while trying to climb the outside walls. The pharaoh's revenge, or the curse of the mummy?

The moment we got off the bus, a band of brigands,

in the form of souvenir sellers, descended on us like a pack of ravening wolves. Everywhere we went, they followed, rattling strings of beads and charms under our noses. They left me alone eventually after I put to use some Arabic I'd found necessary to add to my vocabulary. '*Em shee*,' I told them, which, politely translated, means, 'Take a walk!'

I tramped over the hot sand to the Great Pyramid, and joined the throng who had paid their money for the privilege of descending a passage one hundred metres long into a dark four-thousand-year-old tomb thirty metres below the ground. This is not for those with a fear of enclosed spaces. (It has its moments for the non-claustrophobic as well, I can assure you.) Up a sloping wooden ladder I went, bending over double to negotiate the narrow entrance and creep along a tunnel into the bowels of the earth. Air comes in through shafts in two of the walls, but there wasn't much of it in the passages. The pharaoh doesn't need air, and the builders hadn't catered for visitors.

After what seemed like miles of near-asphyxiation, we came to the two burial chambers built in the pyramid and, further down along the connecting passages, another that had been cut into the rock below. Although the pyramids are huge outside, they are almost solid, and the tombs take up only a relatively tiny space inside, even though they also, before being looted, contained the pharaoh's goods and treasures for his use in the afterworld. The ancient Egyptians believed utterly in eternal life. They believed that the pharaoh was a son of the gods and therefore the bearer of the *Ka*, or life force, and that he left the *Ka* behind in the pyramid after he took off. I could feel something lurking there in the dark musty air. Maybe that's what it was.

The pyramids impressed me, but it was *Abu Hol*, 'The

Father of Terror' – the Sphinx – which surpassed everything I saw. It is surrounded by magical mystery. The sands of the desert concealed it from the world for aeons, and its origin and purpose are long forgotten, but it still inspires homage. Its massive head was silhouetted against the blue sky as it loomed over us gaping tourists below. I had not imagined it would be so huge. Seventy metres long and twenty metres high, it is carved almost completely from the same limestone block and the same kind of stone as Cheops's pyramid. Its face is supposed to be that of Pharaoh Chephren, obviously a most inscrutable fellow.

By now the sun was blazing overhead and the glare bounced of the brightness of the beige desert. It is a long trip around the other sites and, not relishing the idea of hours spent on foot, I thought it best to hire a camel. A large number of these ships of the desert stood around with their owners, tarted up in multi-coloured rugs and tassels – the camels that is. For a small fee the faint-hearted can take pictures rather than ride. I got on a camel which turned out to be like all his brethren: bad-tempered, stubborn, malodorous and possessed of some revolting personal habits. I am not particularly partial to camels, but the horses, which were the alternative transport, looked so tired and hot I didn't have the heart to jump on one.

I hired a car and driver another day and we set off to visit Saqqara, the city of the dead. Here the Step pyramid sat alone, without the touts and hawkers of Giza, on the yellow sand of the desert. It is thought to be the first pyramid built, and the oldest stone edifice of its size in the world.

My driver, whose name was Frouzi – it takes great effort

for me to refrain from comment on this – got the sulks because I wouldn't let him be my official guide, but it was a luxury to be left alone to contemplate. The Step pyramid was the burial place of Pharaoh Zoser and was built by Imhotep, Zoser's chief architect, surgeon and scientist. Imhotep was later deified, and is still regarded as one of the first great men of science and medicine.

Originally the pyramid had been surrounded by an enormous ornate wall, but now only part of it remains. In its great court is a frieze of cobras – tokens of the pharaohs – pictured with hoods erect. In an underground cavern I saw the canopic jars, in which the pharaoh's internal organs were preserved. These, and one of his leg bones found nearby in the desert, are all that remain of him, as the tomb was robbed in ancient times. (I wonder if he is hopping mad about this.) On one of the tomb's outer walls I read the oldest tourist graffiti in the world: words of praise to the pharaoh written by twelfth-century BC visitors from Thebes.

Frouzi, who had by now forgiven me – he was, like most of his countrymen, naturally exuberant and happy – drove a short distance further on so that I could visit the lovely tomb of the Princess Idut, which had several chambers decorated with animals: gazelles, hippopota-muses and cows. I also found the tomb of Ankhma-Hor, which had graphic illustrations of surgical operations and instruments – some obviously for use in circumcisions and others possibly for removal of ingrown toe nails – and the temple of Bubasteion, dedicated to the cat-goddess Bastet, which contained a host of little bandaged bodies – mummified cats. The sight of these made me homesick for William, the big old anti-social tabby who has owned me for many years, although I was sure that even these cat worshippers wouldn't have impressed him.

At Saqqara I also saw the tombs of the sacred Apis bulls, the focus of a major animal cult. The bulls were worshipped as gods in the temple, and when they died they were mummified and put in massive black granite sarcophaguses, then entombed in underground caverns. These caverns are two hundred metres long and are full of mummified falcons, baboons, and ibis, as well as the bulls.

A disreputable-looking old Bedu, proclaiming himself the official guide, was stationed outside. I wasn't going in there without a light, so I rented him and his flickering lamp to escort me through this eerie place. Walking between the rows of huge sarcophaguses containing the remains of the bulls, my scalp tingled. This was a place where ghosts walked behind you.

9 Lost, stolen, killed

Back in Cairo, I concentrated on my means of onward travel. My efforts to book a journey south by river to Luxor and Aswan proved futile. The boats that carry passengers sail at infrequent intervals and a berth is difficult to arrange unless you are prepared to wait several weeks. I enquired also about the steamer from Aswan to Wadi Halfa, just over the Egyptian border in Sudan. My guide book gave the address of a transport company that allegedly sold tickets for this trip. When I presented myself at its office, however, and tendered money to buy one, the staff denied the steamer's very existence. 'No, no,' they assured me repeatedly, 'there is no such thing.' I tried several other companies, but the answer was the same. No one was prepared to admit that there was a Nile steamer taking passengers from Aswan to Wadi Halfa. I began to wonder if this was a conspiracy. Was it another case of 'nobody goes that way'? Perhaps I did not appear a suitable person to be sold a ticket.

Giving the idea of booking a steamer passage in Cairo up as a dead loss, I opted for the train to Aswan via Luxor, feeling sure that I would be able to find the boat to Sudan once I got there. My friends in Saudi had told me that there was a train from Wadi Halfa which went to Khartoum. Once there, I planned to make my way overland to the coast of Africa where I hoped to find a ship going to Asia or Australia.

I set out in search of the Australian Embassy and, I hoped, a visa for Sudan. I had tried phoning for information, but that had been a fiasco. It was virtually impossible to get a connection by phone from the hotel and, as I had already found, even worse trying to master a public phone. There were few available, except in the lobbies of big hotels, and even then special tokens were necessary. They were hard to come by.

The receptionist at my hotel had said he didn't have any. 'You should use the phone in your room,' he'd said.

'I can't get through on it, or I would,' I'd replied testily.

This news hadn't surprised him in the least. He'd given me a dreamy smile and said soothingly, *'Bukra, enshall'ah*, it may be better.'

God willing or not, I hadn't wanted to wait until tomorrow, so I was pursuing the matter in person.

I'd discovered from the travel agent at the Hilton hotel that, to obtain a visa to enter Sudan, you first had to produce a letter from the representative of your country. I learned later that this was the Sudanese way of exempting themselves from responsibility for whatever ill fortune might befall you in their country. Because of war in the south and rebel activity generally, travellers were being told they could visit Sudan only at their own risk.

The Australian Embassy was on the Corniche el Nil, several kilometres up river from the hotel. It took me over an hour in a taxi to find it because of the traffic and the inability of the taxi-driver to understand what I wanted.

After a long delay in a reception area with all the charm of a dentist's waiting room, I was ushered in to meet the consul, a friendly Australian man who was appalled when I said I wanted to travel to Wadi Halfa by boat and from there by train to Khartoum. He said, 'This is not for you. You can't go that way. I have seen men who went as far as Wadi Halfa and turned back at the sight of the train.'

He said a lot more in this vein, and seemed rather alarmed when his arguments only made me more determined to go. I was not passing up the chance of one of the world's great train rides, 1600 kilometres across the Nubian desert to Khartoum. The consul said a lot about bandits in the desert, war in the south, and trains being blown up by terrorists, but I persevered, and in the end he gave in, saying that he would have to ask me to sign a waiver releasing him from any responsibility for whatever might befall me. Then he gave me an official letter to the Sudanese government exempting it from any repercussions. I was on my own. If I got into trouble no one was going to help me or be blamed for it – be it on my head alone if I got myself killed! I wonder if he slipped out secretly for a quick wash of his hands after the manner of P. Pilate. On top of all this doom and gloom, adding insult to injury, I was asked to pay twenty-two Egyptian pounds for the privilege of having my country disown me.

I walked out to the Corniche, clutching my hard-won letter, to find that it was lunchtime and the shops and offices were closing for their two-hour siesta. By now I desperately needed fortifying, so I repaired to Cleopatras, a restaurant on the Nile, to soothe myself with fresh Nile perch and *baba ghanough*, mashed eggplant with *tahina*. Belly dancers perform here, but I decided that I hadn't progressed far enough in my lessons with Alfat and Fifi to ask for a job.

I returned to Shepheard's to ask the staff to direct me to the Sudanese Embassy. One of the difficulties of finding your way around in an Arabic country, if you cannot read Arabic, is looking up addresses in the phone book. Another problem, in Egypt in particular, is that over fifty per cent of the population are illiterate or almost so, and taxi drivers cannot read addresses even when you've had them written for you in Arabic.

The hotel staff sent me to the gate house of an immense faded villa in one of the wide tree-shaded streets of Garden City, where the upper crust lived in colonial days (and some still do), in fine old Georgian and Victorian mansions overlooking the Nile. Most of these once gracious buildings are now neglected and decaying and their huge grounds contain only the tangled remnants of gardens.

In the street outside the villa I joined an extremely long line of Sudanese-looking men who seemed to be obtaining work permits. I made it to the office window after two hours of shuffling forward, only to find I needed five copies of the visa application form, plus five photographs of myself. This was far more than usual for a visa, but I guess they were expecting to need lots for when I became lost, stolen or killed, as they seemed sure I would be.

I went looking for a photographer. By the time I returned with the photos and rejoined the line, the office had shut. The next day I returned to the fray and, after half a morning in the queue, was finally told that I was in the wrong place, unless I wanted to wait for two to four weeks for my application to be considered. The official, a dusty specimen reclining in a wooden sentry box, suggested I take myself to the embassy proper, as this office was only a branch that dealt with expatriate workers.

An hour in a taxi later I found the embassy, absolutely miles away in the outer suburbs, which in Cairo seem to stretch to infinity. The staff seemed surprised by my application, and I gathered they did not receive many tourist applications for visas. But they didn't try to deter me. I got the distinct impression that they thought I was flying to Khartoum from Cairo, a misapprehension I did not try to correct.

My visa application was finally lodged, but I could not, of course, get it that same day. Such haste would have been uncouth. I went back next day, collected my visa and proceeded on to the train station to make a booking on the night train to Aswan via a stop in Luxor, from where, *en shal'lah*, I could catch the Nile steamer for Wadi Halfa.

At Rameses train station I was boomeranged from window to window for two hours before I was able to buy a ticket to Aswan. It would have been longer but, after watching Egyptian women push their way in front of men to be served first, and knowing that this was accepted, even expected, behaviour, I did it too. A first-class sleeper, with sole occupancy of the cabin, was reserved for me. Once, in Russia, I had failed to ask for sole occupancy and ended up sharing my night's rest with a large Russian gent who had some most peculiar ideas of what sharing a cosy little cabin included, and I made sure that wouldn't happen this time.

I came out of the train station and strolled in the direction, I thought, of my hotel, enjoying the unusual sights and sounds of the streets. Then, quite by accident, I happened upon the Cosmopolitan hotel. I had read about this grand old place, and wanted to visit it, but hadn't been able to work out where it was. It was now down-at-heel, but still housed great chandeliers, lead-lighted and stained glass windows and doors, an old leather bar and twenty-foot-high ceilings and windows. I went into the massive dining room and lunched, all alone, amidst tattered grandeur.

10 Star of Egypt

The night train to Aswan, formerly the famous *Star of Egypt*, is an overnight sleeper and one of the world's classic train journeys. It is now called, less romantically, the *Egyptian Train de Luxe*, and leaves Rameses station at seven in the evening, arriving in Aswan the next day around mid-morning, and at Luxor a little before. It is air-conditioned and has compartments with two sleeping berths, which convert to comfortable seats during the day, a wash basin, hot and cold water and a wardrobe.

I boarded the train in plenty of time to investigate its possibilities before it pulled out of the station. The toilets down the corridor were communal and filthy, which is usual for Egypt. The windows were filthy too. I found a bar car but no restaurant, and was devastated until a cheery steward told me that meals are included in the fare and would be served in my compartment. Any deficiency in funds this caused the train company was made up for by the horrendous price of the tea and bottled water I was forced to buy. It would have been courting disaster to drink water from the tap.

After a solitary dinner I went to explore the bar car, where I found a jolly crowd already making merry. And they got progressively jollier as the night wore on. They included a mixed bag of nationalities, but a large contingent was made up of a party of French tourists, some of whom ended up dancing with the waiters, the barmen and the other help to the traditional wailing Egyptian music being played non-stop at deafening pitch. Not much can be done to this music but a sort of eastern belly dance: a waltz would be out of the question. Before long someone jumped up onto a table and the party really started to liven up. It was all good fun. As we rattled and jolted our way through the Egyptian night, I held onto the bar and talked (or shouted) to several young British army officers who said they were stationed in Cairo.

It was very late by the time I wove my way to my sleeper. I fell on the bed and was almost concussed by my pillow. It seemed to be stuffed with a tree trunk. The mattress was worse, paper-thin and hard as nails. I used my rolled-up jumper as a pillow and slept quite well.

The next morning I threw up my window blind and there was Egypt spread out before me. The Egyptian countryside was just as I had always imagined it; the green of the Nile valley with a distinct contrast between the rich river banks and the desert. Sometimes we left the riverside and went through a stretch of desert, an expanse of undulating gold exactly like those I'd seen in picture books.

The fields and cultivated areas came right up to the train line, which followed the river closely. We passed through tiny mud-brick villages where rural life continues in almost the same way as is pictured on the walls of the tombs. Against the blue sky I saw camels being used to load goods and move railway trucks and carriages, while on paths along the water's edge a farmer or two would be leading grey donkeys laden with produce in large woven cane panniers, one on each flank. Some passed so close I could have touched them, had the window not been sealed for the benefit of the air-conditioning. Peasants, the *fellahin*, dressed in *galabayas* and turbans, were tilling their fields, forking hay or ploughing with teams of donkeys. Women or boys tended herds of sheep and goats, with the desert or bare hills as a back-drop. On the roads camels or donkeys pulled old wooden carts and drays.

At the riverside women were washing clothes and collecting water in earthenware pots, which they carried home on their heads. Lush grass grew along the banks of the irrigation ditches, and on both sides they were planted with crops or date palms, which in places over-hung both sides to form a cool sylvan tunnel. Dates hung under the fronds of the palms in great bunches, and I was surprised to see that they were bright, large, reddish and juicy, not the wizened dark brown items I had encountered as a child in my mother's kitchen.

11 City of the dead

Early that morning the *Train de Luxe* arrived at Luxor, which lies along the left bank of the river Nile. On the station platform I passed the French tourists, some of whom looked decidedly worse for wear after their previous night's revelry. I refrained from asking after their health. School-girl French with an excruciating accent would have been too cruel at that time of the day.

Luxor, the Thebes of ancient times, can trace its origins back four thousand years to a village that prospered on this site. Visitors have been coming to gaze and wonder at the temples of Luxor, Karnak, Rameses II, Hatshepsut, and other superbly preserved masterpieces, for thousands of years. Greeks and Romans were the first, and in the nineteenth century British and other European tourists started to winter here. Ancient monuments, Victoriana and Art Deco exist side by side. Not much has changed since the British left forty years ago. My hotel – the Savoy – was reminiscent of the days of the Charleston and flappers.

My guide book described Luxor as 'redolent with the odour of horse'. And it was. The streets were generously decorated with their calling cards. The poor horses often looked uncared for, but they were considerably cheaper than taxis. I weighed the cruelty of making the miserable beasts haul me around town against the money they would earn for food. As always with me, the food argument won.

There are only three major streets in Luxor; they are all unpaved dirt, and the sparse traffic on them is mostly horse and bicycle. I felt at once the change of pace after Cairo. Even though its population is now over 100,000, Luxor still feels like a large village. I wandered behind the Corniche and entered a maze of small streets and convoluted alleys through which the call to prayer reverberated. Among the mud-brick houses, *souks* and mosques, swags of unmentionables swung from upper storey laundry lines. I stopped dead in my tracks in front of a restaurant with a sign unashamedly declaring it to be 'Shiti'! I didn't eat there.

The next morning I crossed by ferry to the opposite side of the river to visit the City of the Dead, where pharaohs and noblemen were buried, mostly in the isolated Valley of the Kings, and where workmen, priests, artisans and temple guards once lived. (A contradiction in terms?)

This side of the river is barren and bleak, and the sun bounces off it with stupendous heat. The tombs on the visiting list are far apart, and you have to make a steep climb to each of them. This is no outing for your average couch potato. Deciding that walking was only for masochists, I hired a taxi, ignoring the solicitations of the owners of mini-donkeys. The area certainly earns its name of the City of the Dead. After a few hours I was ready to join them. But the tombs were worth it. The valley contains sixty-two of them, the entrance to each being a long steep tunnel hewn into the rock, ending in an antechamber to the burial chamber. The walls of the tombs were covered with paintings and inscriptions from

The Book of the Dead, formulae which could procure you a passage to the after-life. *That* book must have been a best-seller.

Rameses IX's walls were painted with animals, snakes and demons, and Rameses VI's had a scene, spread across the ceiling, of the goddess Nut in the sky; darkest blue with myriads of stars for the night sky and bright azure for the day. The freshness of the colours and life emanating from the paintings made me shiver, as though I was communing with the artist who had stood on this spot and left behind a part of himself four thousand years ago. I realised that the ancients were right. There *is* immortality.

This tomb of Rameses VI saved Tutankhamun's tomb, the only one ever found intact, from plunder. Tutankhamun's tomb had been built beneath it, and the robbers had not realised there was another on the same site. The walls of Tutankhamun's tomb are also decorated with the words he needed to say for admission to eternity. I hope he made it.

In the tomb of Amenophis II, the king sleeps on in his stone sarcophagus where he was placed at his death, a garland of flowers still around his neck. It is an extraordinary feeling to be looking at flowers that are over two thousand years old, far more impressive for me than all the jewels and paintings.

Past the Valley of the Kings is the Valley of the Queens, where there are seventy-five excavated tombs of queens and children of pharaohs. The nine-year-old son of Rameses III, Amunherkhepshep (try saying that six times quickly), lies here. He died when his mother was five months pregnant, and the pain of her mourning was so great that she miscarried. A pathetic little mummy rests in the sarcophagus, where it was buried with its brother.

Further out again in the foothills are the tombs of the nobles where there are about four hundred burial sites. But I'd had enough of death by now, so I left them in peace.

Another morning I crossed again by ferry to the opposite side of the river to see the temple of Queen Hatshepsut. Rounding a corner of this splendid monument I came upon a strange sight; a large elderly female English tourist laid out like a fish on a slab of fallen marble. Ever the Florence of Arabia, I went to the rescue. I rounded up some strong men and a blanket for them to carry her in, and we man-handled her to a taxi, then to her tour bus, and finally across the river to her hotel. This difficult manoeuvre took two hours, for most of which time she lay with her head in my lap. The poor old dear was violently sick several times, and I was unable to avoid coming into intimate contact with a good deal of her lunch.

Twenty-four hours later I began to feel decidedly strange. I took my temperature and it was forty-two degrees. Not long after I was floored by a particularly foul type of Egyptian plague. I knew I was extremely ill, but I would not risk the dubious ministrations of the Egyptian medical fraternity or, worse yet, a hospital – not with the inside information I had on them from Saudi. I couldn't leave my room for three days; I could hardly get out of bed. My temperature remained around forty-two and I had all the symptoms of cholera.

The room 'boy', a big old Nubian clad in a long caftan and massive white turban, came hourly to put his hand on my forehead. He brought me a steady stream of tea and bottled water, and rubbed my head with lemon juice, claiming that was a sure cure for what ailed me. I treated myself as best I could and lived on crackers, bananas and copious fluids. My intake quickly converted to output and it was hard to maintain a positive fluid balance, but I knew that was all I had to do to survive, so I did. Four days later I decided I might live. I had become stronger and could get up for a while, even though someone had replaced my knee joints with cotton wool, but more days passed before I dared to leave the safety of the toilet. Little by little I extended the time I could absent myself from the vicinity of the loo, until I managed to take a horse carriage to the train station to book a seat on the next day's train to Aswan.

I don't know whether it was the lemon juice, but the cure was highly effective. That was the last sick day I have had up until now. I have made a vow, however, that all the elderly English ladies in the world can lie prostrate about the ruins of Egypt, and I will never help one up again. Mother always told me not to pick things up in the street. Now I know why.

12 Jewel of the Nile

At Aswan I stayed in a hilltop hotel called the Nile City, supposedly a two-star establishment. How it achieved those two stars was a wonder – its rooms were spartan and its amenities strictly basic – but the folk were kind and helpful. It was owned and run by Nubians, cost nine dollars a day including breakfast, lunch, taxes and tips (a week here cost about the same as a night at Shepheard's), and had a wonderful high location, with gardens overlooking the river. My single room was very small, but quite adequate once I had adjusted myself and the furniture, as is my wont. A sign behind the door informed me that 'breakfast is compulsory' – you must enjoy yourself! – and also offered 'companionable' baths, which I couldn't wait to try.

Aswan, the southernmost of Egyptian cities, is the gateway to Africa and Nubia and has been a market town and traditional meeting place on the great caravan routes for centuries. The word 'Aswan' is derived from the Arabic word for trade. Caravans of camels and elephants brought slaves, ivory, gold, spices and semi-precious stones here to be sold, bartered and haggled over. Traders from all over the world still come to Aswan, although the only caravans that now sway into the *souks* are the strings of camels brought for sale from Sudan.

In the nineteenth century Aswan became popular as

a winter resort for the British and the rich and famous from nearby countries. King Farouk spent the cooler months of the year in his palace here during his reign, presumably eating chickens, and Mohommed Shah Agha Khan, the forty-eighth Imam, or leader, of the sect of the Ismaili Islam, was so fond of Aswan that he chose it for the site of his tomb. After his death in 1957 his wife, the Begum Khan, built a white Cararra marble mausoleum on the hillside of the west bank above his villa. The Begum still lives there for part of the year, and every day she places one red rose on his sarcophagus, a ritual the gardener performs when she is away.

Aswan is lovely. The jewel colours of the river, its many bright dotted islands and rocks among little white rapids and waterfalls, the graceful sails of the *feluccas* against the periwinkle sky and the sensational fiery sunsets combine to create a scene of tranquil beauty. My favourite stop on the Corniche was the old ex-British rowing club, where I would sit on the wide verandah, sip tea and watch the boats. Sometimes a snake charmer would come along and dump his basket with its resident cobra on the footpath and, for a few piastres, play a flute to lure his repulsive accomplice out for the tourists to goggle at. I would have gladly paid him to keep its dubious charms to himself.

The town consists mostly of mazes of lanes and alleys full of houses and *souks*. Aswan does not depend so much on tourism as Luxor, and the markets are mostly for the locals. Wandering by myself among the stalls, I found people buying spices, perfume, meat, vegetables, pots, pans and plastic ware. I was a curiosity to the locals, but they were always friendly. It was a pleasant change not to have tourist junk shoved in my face. I bought fruit, which was plentiful and cheap. Mandarin oranges were especially nice. But I tried to avoid the meat market, with its great slabs of unappealing, evil-smelling meat and obscenely naked carcasses hanging in the open and subject to the attentions of the local flying insect population.

I once found myself in a similar meat market in Sumatra. I was with my sister, Annie, who has led a more sheltered existence than I have, and had the unpleasant experience of watching her turn green. When she began to make gurgling noises indicating the imminent eruption of her breakfast, I dragged her hurriedly from the scene.

In the late afternoon I liked to visit the Old Cataract hotel, which stands high above the river in an abundance of greenery. The exterior of the Old Cataract was used in the film of Agatha Christie's *Death On the Nile* and she is said to have written some of the book here. Inside it is Art Nouveau grandeur and elegance, with a bevelled glass lift, lofty ceilings, polished wood floors and solid antique furniture.

Taking a *felucca* I would sail over to its landing and climb what seemed like several thousand steps up to the terrace bar. I was in desperate need of its bounty by the time I made it. Then, sitting on the shaded verandah with a drink, I would watch the sun set against a background of sails moving on blue water and the glittering white of the Agha Khan's tomb on the opposite river bank.

13 Nefertiti

After a few days enjoying Aswan, I set out on my mission of finding the riverboat to Sudan and buying a ticket for its next voyage. I asked my hotel staff for directions and was put in a taxi clutching an address written in Arabic on a scrap of paper. We ended up not at the shipping company, but with a shopkeeper who was supposed to know how to point me in the right direction. Three stops later, I finally came to rest in the office of the agency that sold tickets for the boat: 'The Nile Valley Navigational Office' or the 'Sudanese Maritime Office', they answered to both.

The agent, an overweight, genial soul, surveyed me with a mixture of amusement and alarm and did his level best to dissuade me from such foolishness. At my mention of Wadi Halfa, he exclaimed, echoing the words of the Australian consul in Cairo, 'It is not for you. Nobody goes that way.' I persisted, however, and he gave in, saying he would see what he could do, and that I should come back tomorrow. I did, and was surprised to discover that he actually had a ticket for me.

I reminded him that I wanted a first-class cabin, alone, and was assured that this was what I had. The boat, he vowed, was the big, new one called *Nefertiti* after the queen of fabled beauty, took only twenty hours, *en shal'lah*, and the price of the ticket included eight cups of tea.

'But what about food?' I asked, ever mindful of the priorities. He said there was a dining room.

I paid up and he gave me instructions about the time and place to present myself for boarding. He shook my hand fervently and, offering words of encouragement, led me to the door and saw me off rather like a priest seeing a prisoner to the electric chair. I departed with his invocations for the protection of Allah following me.

At the appointed hour I took a taxi to the landing site, an hour's drive south of Aswan, where the river became once more navigable. My first sight of the ship was not encouraging. If this was the big new one, heaven help all those in peril on the deep in the little old ones. She skulked there at anchor, sullenly rusting away in the sunlight, a woebegone example of navigable (I hoped) junk. Queen Nefertiti must be doing cart-wheels in her tomb. This ship made the *Al Lhara* look like a floating palace, and I regretted now that I'd had the temerity to sneer at my former transport. Well, I was being justly punished for my sins.

The *Nefertiti* was unbelievably, unspeakably dirty and decrepit. But she was not alone in her misery. She swarmed with bodies dragging huge bundles aboard and laying claim to the bit of deck they would occupy for the jaunt to Wadi Halfa.

The taxi driver and I, who were old friends by now – after an hour in the company of any Egyptian it was hard (for me, anyway) not to be – struggled with my mountainous suitcase to the dockside, where we were taken in tow by a beaming member of the Nubian crew. He was tall, strong and handsome with very black skin: typical of his race who are neither Arab nor Negro, but unique to this north-east corner of the African continent. After a great deal of confusion and several false stops, he deposited me in a minute, dreary dungeon masquerading as a first-class cabin. I was relieved to see that it contained only an upper and lower bunk and no other occupant, and disseminated my travelling accoutrements about liberally. Then I went up on deck to watch the fun (and pandemonium) of setting sail, which was, naturally, an hour late.

When I returned to the cabin I found that I was no longer alone. A young Sudanese woman had commandeered the lower bunk and moved all my belongings to the upper one. I thought that she had made a mistake and showed her my ticket. She looked blank. Her brother, who was escorting her, spoke English, and he explained that my ticket was only for half the cabin. Oh well, at least she was female and there was only one of her. I had no idea what was written on the ticket except the numbers. It could have said that I was to stoke the boilers for all I could tell. It was quite likely that the shipping agent hadn't believed I really wanted two beds to myself, when it was utter luxury in Middle-Eastern travel to have *one* bed to yourself. So he had charged me for two and sold the other one anyway. I do not get in a stew about things I cannot change, so I went to find some eats.

I had been told by the agent and other tour people that there was no need to bring food for any part of the journey between Aswan and Khartoum. They said that there was a dining room on the ship, plenty of food in Wadi Halfa, and meals available on the train. Later I realised that none of them had ever seen the train, or even the ship, and they were simply telling me what I wanted to hear. The truth would have been a whole lot more useful.

From the boat, the Nile was a wide, brown, calm river, at times giving way to marshes and swamps scattered with clumps of floating weed. Several times we passed boats and barges going in the opposite direction towards Aswan. They were loaded down to the gunwales, goods and people stacked all over them, and they cleared the water by only a few inches, perilously close to sinking.

The *Nefertiti* had a deck class, a second class consisting of wooden seats on the deck, and a few tiny cabins labelled, by someone with a warped sense of humour, first class. The cabins would have accommodated a maximum of twenty-eight people. There was a bathroom with hole-in-the-floor toilets, but no ablution facilities. The tiled floor was awash with water and goodness knows what else. When it got rough, the hole was hard to hit. A forty-four gallon drum of water and a dipper, serving in lieu of toilet paper in the traditional Middle-Eastern manner, added to the mess.

Passengers were packed solid on the decks in every conceivable space. I got up in the middle of the night to go to the bathroom, and had to step over many sleeping bodies in the narrow corridor. They were obviously deck-class passengers who had crept inside to escape the cold. I didn't envy them their sleeping quarters. The smell from the toilets was vile, and the overflow ran out the door in noisome trickles. Those left outside on the deck, however, must have been frozen stiff. I wonder how they survived. Most of them seemed to have few clothes.

The alleged dining room, a large dark place on the top deck and the only public room on the ship, had never heard of food. Horror! Tea was what the ticket said and tea was what they served. Eight cups and free, perhaps, but not what I had envisaged for my dinner. By luck I had some cracker biscuits, a hand of bananas and the essential bottled water in my bag.

I had company in my privation. Five other westerners

already sat on a bench in front of one of the long wooden tables by the time I arrived. They stared dismally at their glasses of a dark liquid impersonating tea. The rest of the crowd in the room were Sudanese, with a sprinkling of Egyptians. Three of the westerners were Finnish, a girl and two boys, who were backpackers travelling in the normal unkempt manner of that breed. The other two were a married German couple, also backpacking, of the elderly hippy persuasion. They were a little cleaner than the Finns, but still retained the aura of having slept in haystacks.

It puzzles me that backpackers generally are like this, as though it is a badge of courage to look as awful as possible. I was wearing my usual travelling kit: my Good Little Woman outfit, consisting of an extremely boring, but terribly respectable, long sleeved shirt, baggy slacks and sensible shoes. Tried and tested on many customs and immigration officials around the world, it has only failed once to produce a smooth entry to whatever country I've tried to invade. That country was Saudi Arabia and doesn't count. They don't know respectable when they see it.

14 Wadi Halfa

We landed near Wadi Halfa and I felt that I was seeing Africa for the first time. Egypt, although technically part of Africa, had not seemed in any way African to me; it has a character all its own. The boat had come out of Lake Nasser at the point where the Nile leaves the lake to become once more a river, and we soon arrived at a landing on a bend, and the end of our journey.

According to the shipping agent's schedule, we should have arrived at ten in the morning, but we actually got to the landing at about noon. This was very punctual for the Middle East, but absolutely stupendous by African standards. The landing place did not have a wharf or quay, just the remains of two old landing barges floating at the water's edge. The boat simply tied up to the outermost one, and passengers had to teeter to the shore across both of them. They provided the only flat area on which goods and people could be landed, for high, sand-coloured cliffs rose up immediately at the river's edge. On the ridges of these cliffs sat, in various states of repose, dozens of men, who had obviously come to watch the entertainment. They were clad in a motley collection of *galabayas* and all manner of ragged and tatty coats, cloaks and head-dresses, with the exception of one terribly smart chap who sported a bright red, knitted, woollen beanie. The landscape was totally devoid of vegetation and, except for the number of people, could have been a portrait of the end of the earth.

Local excuses for taxis were lined up at the top of the cliffs, at the beginning of a steep slope away from the river. They included several huge antiquated trucks in the most appalling state of disrepair, and some strange jeep-type vehicles, also battered antiques. Some must have been made in the 1930s: nothing was newer than 1940.

My cabin on the ship had a porthole looking directly on the place where people were going ashore. Knowing, from sad experience, that the accepted method of exiting would be one mad stampede, and not wanting to get caught in it, I sat and watched and waited until the worst rush subsided. This took about an hour and a half.

The Sudanese bring back from Egypt whatever they can manage to carry, drag, push or heave, either for themselves, or their relatives, or to sell. They lugged tied-up bundles of pots and pans, washing baskets, plastic buckets, even a kitchen sink! The passengers who had inside cabins threw these bundles out of their doors and pushed them along the tiny corridor, clogging the entire exit. The *Nefertiti* was licensed and equipped to carry only two hundred passengers, but the ship's officer told me that there had been over seven hundred on board.

At last, at about half past one, the throng cleared enough to allow me to manoeuvre my suitcase into the corridor. For once I was not embarrassed by its size, because it was tiny alongside the baggage some of the locals were toting.

I looked around for help with The Monster, and spied a hopeful-looking candidate – his hands were empty and his *galabaya* hitched up ready for action. There are no official porters, since few people in a country this poor are prepared to pay someone to do what they can do themselves. I learned as I went along that if I wanted assistance the only thing to do was to approach someone who looked a possibility and ask for help. They generally agreed. My porter and I settled upon twenty Sudanese pounds as payment for the pleasure of his company on to Sudanese soil. I thought it was cheap, at a couple of Australian dollars, to get my bag ferried a long way across the landing barges and up a very steep incline. I never could have negotiated the path with my bag, but my wiry helper skipped away quite unconcerned.

The Monster lumbered off on the back of the porter and I followed. We made it through the ship, down the stairs, across the deck, down the gang-plank and on to the first landing barge to immigration.

The customs and immigration departments were housed in a collection of what, in all honesty, could not be called sheds. They were really just huts. On the first landing barge was the immigration hut, on the second was the first stage of customs, and finally you entered another tin shack to fill out the essential currency form. For the compulsory payment of a Sudanese pound, you were given a pink exit form which supposedly had to be produced when you left the country. No one ever asked for mine.

At immigration I caused quite a stir. The officials were amazed by the apparition of such a staid-looking tourist way out here. And not only female, but alone! When I told them I had come to visit Sudan because I had heard about it from Sudanese friends I had been working with in Saudi Arabia, they were absolutely delighted. They had not been unpleasant to begin with – the Sudanese are charming and gracious people – but after this they were covered with smiles, saying, '*Adlan Wasalam Sudan*' ('Welcome to Sudan'), and more felicitations along that line. My fame spread before me and at customs I was greeted with more welcomes, followed by, 'And what have you got in your bag? Nothing that's not for your own use, is it? No? No! Well, right then, off you go and the peace of Allah go with you.'

The same happened in the next hut, where a currency statement was required. The form you fill out, declaring how much money you have, has to be produced on leaving the country and all transactions have to be recorded on it during your stay. There is an extremely active black market between Sudan and Egypt and customs and currency control check stringently to see that Sudanese returning home do not have contraband or items on which duty should be paid. Customs are strict with their own people and they usually look askance at foreigners, thinking they might be carrying *bangar* (marijuana), or undeclared money. I had, of course, quantities of prohibited American dollars and Egyptian pounds secreted about my person.

In the customs shed I passed the backpackers, who had left the ship with the first wave two hours ago. Their bags were flung open on the floor and all their belongings strewn about. Everything had been stripped down and searched to the last seam. I must have appeared quite daft to them, with my square clothes, my umbrella, my whacking great suitcase and my man to carry it.

At the top of the cliff I was accosted by a flock of taxi drivers and illegal currency peddlers, all eager to change cash money for me. This was directly in the line of vision of the official currency department, to whom I had just declared I had nothing but travellers' cheques with me. Everyone else seemed to ignore the officials, so I joined in a bit of black marketeering.

I turned my attention to transport to the town and

negotiated for a 'taxi'. It was a ramshackle 1939 truck of obscure model, held together by fencing wire. I could not have cared less about the mode of travel, as I fondly imagined I was going to be taken to a hotel where I would be cleaned and fed. The tour people had all said, 'Oh, yes, there are hotels in Wadi Halfa, lots of hotels, good ones and bad ones, but lots of them.'

I sat in the windowless and windscreen-less front seat of the truck receiving proposals of marriage: only three, I must admit, but then I was only there for three quarters of an hour and wasn't looking my best. I was plainly a millionaire and a fool to boot – I had given ten pounds for the privilege of riding in the front seat of this rusting relic of the pre-war years – and was therefore wonderfully eligible in the marriage stakes. I *had* thought that a dollar was not too much to pay for the luxury of the front seat, compared to paying ten cents to squat in the uncovered back among the dust, heat and mass of other passengers.

We set off only when not another soul could be shoehorned in. I'd noticed that all the vehicles were parked on the crest of the hill with their noses pointing down, and I realised now the logistics of this. Our truck had no starter motor. To commence our journey, the driver released the handbrake and, with the help of a few bystanders, we rolled off the top of the hill and the impetus of the vehicle took us away. The old dear lumbered away downhill until its valiant, geriatric engine coughed, wheezed and *roared* into life. Actually, it was more like death – it sounded as sick as all get out. I had instant memories of the ancient and unroadworthy vehicles of Burma, my favourite place in all the world.

Away we chugged, raising a great cloud of dust behind us. There was no proper road, merely a track like the ones found in the middle of the Australian outback, with great ruts, holes and sandbogs. I prayed that the poor engine would not seize up, because if it did there would be no one other than the passengers to push-start the beast again. Obviously it ran on People Power. Re-starting it would have been tricky, because there were no more hills, only dead flat sand.

As far as could be seen the country all around was desert: sand, sand, and more sand. Every now and then a rocky prominence of ancient mien poked up out of the flat ground, as though mountains had been worn down to their initial rock. I found the country very exciting. At last I was not only in Africa for the first time, but also in the desert as I had always imagined it to be.

It was an overcast day with a lot of wind, and the river was grey and drear. The driver told me that this was the cold season, and the sky was always clear when the hot weather came. The people I saw were not dressed to withstand the cold. Nobody seemed to have any warm clothes, and the houses could never be called wind or cold resistant. It seemed a very cruel land to live in, especially if you were poor and ill-nourished, as almost everyone seemed to be.

We chugged along in our auto museum escapee; it coughed, wheezed, spluttered, gurgled and burped. I asked, 'How far?' and was told, 'Only five kilometres, *en shal'lah*.' It may well have been, but we took over an hour to get there. The track did not run in a straight and decent line but weaved here and there, hiccoughed off at tangents and returned crazily in the manner of the proverbial drunken sailor, while the truck lumbered along at the pace of a handicapped snail.

Eventually we came in sight of Wadi Halfa. From a distance it was the real thing; a classic picture from a film about the French Foreign Legion. My soul had searched for this in vain in Saudi Arabia. It's there, but I never got the chance to see it. Here, finally, was the mud-brick walled fort with a palm tree or two standing above it on the skyline. But although Wadi Halfa looked like a walled city from afar, as we drew closer I could see that the walls were actually a series of separate ones around individual buildings, close enough to look continuous from a distance. Wadi Halfa was very big on walls; every building seemed to have one around it. I suppose they were to keep the wild animals out of the family compound, and the goats, camels and donkeys in. All the walls and most of the buildings, with the exception of a few small tin sheds, were built of mud brick. The houses were very basic: single-storeyed, flat-roofed affairs consisting merely of four walls and a roof, completely enclosed by outer walls around a square.

The truck elbowed its unsteady way between two of the walls to a slightly wider bit of track, ground to a halt and stood there rattling and shaking with its engine still running. I wondered why we had stopped here. The Sudanese folk on the back of the truck dismounted and quickly disappeared. The backpackers also got off and looked about. Then someone said to me, 'This is it. This is the town. You get off here.' I was later to discover that this was the main street.

I noticed a tin shed which had a crude sign roughly tacked to its front, informing the world that we were at the Tourist and Customs Office. I explained that I wanted to go to a hotel and was told that this was it. I asked if I could not go to the *big* hotel and the locals said, 'Aiwah! Aiwah! Yes! Yes! This is the big hotel!' They beamed with pride. Of course they had brought me to the best!

Looking again, I saw to the left, behind a mud wall, a low mud building that had nothing to distinguish it from the other hovels. This must be the Big Hotel. My vision of a hot bath grew dimmer. In the meantime, I had obtained the unsolicited company in the front seat of the truck of a most cheerful young Sudanese gent. He seemed to have appointed himself my guide and had attached himself to me, feeling perhaps that I needed a protector. I didn't complain: I could have used one right then. He now told me happily that all the hotels were full. Very well, I thought, I'm not unloading The Monster for nothing. I'll let the backpackers trudge in there and find out. They trekked in dutifully, soon emerging with the news that the hotel was full and there were no vacancies in the town.

Apparently this was as far as the transport went, but I did not get off. I just sat there looking hopeful. The backpackers set off along the track that was rumoured to lead to another hotel. I let the driver and his helper know that they were not putting me off to walk about. I was going to be chauffeured. I convinced the driver that, as I was not English, I did not walk about in the midday sun. He had no way of dislodging me short of brute force, so he drove off in search of somewhere to unload me. The truck, which all this time (understandably) had been kept running, trundled away again and clattered, chuttered, chundered and chugged to the next hotel.

Now I believed that the other *was* the best hotel. Impossible though it seemed, this one looked even more primitive, some sort of cross between a pigsty and a fowl house. I sent in my bodyguard to enquire, but there was no room at this inn either. He came out saying, 'No,' at the next one also, so we bounced on to the next. Unbelievably, they got progressively worse. Meanwhile my guide and protector, who seemed a nice fellow although he had a severe turn in one eye, which made him look as though he had one eye on the mantelpiece and the other up the chimney, had decided I was worth marrying and had proposed to me. I began to wonder if this was the national sport.

There turned out to be only four hotels in Wadi Halfa. I sat firm on the truck and said, 'You have to put me somewhere.' I was not moving from the refuge of its familiar debility. Once on the sand, I would be in a hopeless position, like my friends the backpackers. We kept passing them as they plodded about in the sand with their bags. The driver took me back to the first hotel, the big one. On second inspection, this one looked like a cowshed, but it was an improvement on the pigsty, and was growing handsomer by the minute. My friend and would-be suitor now pronounced himself to be a tourist agent, a vocation which I suspect had come to him since he encountered me on the truck. He said he would put me in the restaurant of the hotel, where I could stay until he found me somewhere to sleep. All ideas of a room of my own had long since fled, and my only object now was a roof over my head.

My suitor dumped me and my belongings in a shed that was half tin and half chicken wire and accommodated a few grotty tables and chairs. This, I was told, was the restaurant.

I looked around to see four young westerners: two Dutch girls travelling together, and two young American men doing likewise. They had come up on the train from Khartoum to catch the boat to Egypt. The girls had found a bed for the night before, but the fellows had slept on the tables in the restaurant. There were also three delightful Korean boys who were studying in Saudi Arabia and travelling around on their holidays. They had also come from Khartoum by train *en route* to Egypt, and had slept on the restaurant tables. The Dutch girls very kindly bought me a cup of tea – my initial thoughts, on hearing that this was a restaurant, had been for food, but on being told that it was not served until evening, I sought other distractions. I sat there sipping the strong black brew heavily laced with sugar, and heard about the situation in Wadi Halfa and the train trip, which apparently had been a nightmare, and one I would have to face soon.

15 Achmed's bed

Wadi Halfa is nothing but a whistle stop, a transit place where the boat from Egypt meets the train from Khartoum and both divest themselves of their throngs. All being well, which it often is not, the train leaves the day after the steamer arrives. The boat goes another day after that. There were approximately four thousand transients in this tiny little dot on the map and that many pass through each week, hard as it is to believe. A tremendous amount of commerce (not to mention smuggling) goes on between Egypt and Sudan, and most of the people travelling this route are trading, doing business, or visiting friends or family, while some are Sudanese students attending the university in Cairo. As both the train and the boat stay overnight or longer before departing, almost all of those people have to stay somewhere and they cope however they can, dossing down in any likely spot. This doesn't seem to bother anyone.

I stayed in the restaurant for more than an hour. In Wadi Halfa there is nothing to look at except the desert, and nothing to do except sit in a shed in the sun drinking sweet tea. Indolence crept over me. I would have been content to remain there inert but, after finishing several cups of tea and listening to everyone's story, I felt that the Great Bed Search should continue. So far I was the only unaccompanied female stranded without a bed, or even a sleeping bag, which everyone else had. Of the Europeans from the boat, the Finnish girl had her two boyfriends, and the German woman her husband, to protect them. In fact, I was the only person I met who was travelling alone. This amazed everyone, even me after I realised what I had got into. It appeared that my would-be sweetheart had given up and deserted me, for he had not returned. I decided, from what I knew of the Islamic code of chivalry towards women and hospitality to travellers, that my best move would be to go to the hotel manager and throw myself upon his mercy.

I found him leaning on a makeshift counter just inside the entrance, and said very politely in my best Arabic, 'The peace of Allah be upon you. I hope you are well today.' He responded in like style and, giving him my most pathetic but honest look, I said, 'Sir, I have a problem. I have nowhere to sleep.'

He began to discuss this, at great length, with three or four other men, while I waited demurely with downcast eyes: the correct procedure for a woman in an Islamic country while men are deciding her fate. Finally they spoke to me and, even with my limited comprehension of Arabic, I understood that I was being offered the manager's bed. Uncertain whether this offer included the manager I gracefully declined, saying, 'Oh, no no. I could not take the bed of the manager, but how kind of you to offer.'

He said, 'Very well. Come outside.'

We trooped outside and found, standing on the verandah, an old, iron-framed bed. It had an obviously secondhand mattress about one inch thick, and an extremely used sheet. The manager said, 'This is Achmed's bed, but you can have it. Come, I will show you where to put it.'

With never a thought as to where poor Achmed would

sleep, I picked up one end of the bed. The manager took the other. We trundled it all around the hotel, in and out of courtyards and across quadrangles, until he found a room he liked, presumably because it looked big enough to accommodate another bed. Then he said, 'Okay. Put it down here.' The room already contained seven beds, all the same as mine (or, more correctly, Achmed's), but we managed to cram it in at the far end in front of a door. He said, 'Okay?' And I said, 'Okay! Lovely. Thank you very much. How very kind. Allah will surely reward such a kind and generous man.'

I meant it. I really was thrilled. The Hilton could not have looked better to me right then, considering that the alternative was sleeping outside or on a table in a restaurant sporting chicken wire for walls. The vision of sleeping in the open had been terrible to contemplate and it could have had disastrous results. I might never have been seen again. By daylight, even alone, I felt quite safe. I could always call upon some good Muslim to help me. But at night, images of a life in the white slave trade assailed me. (Not that they would have kept me long. A couple of days of my bossing them around and they would have returned me for a refund.) It seemed to be acceptable for foreign men and accompanied women to sleep anywhere they could, and all the ones I met had sleeping bags, but imagine sleeping outside without even a blanket on a night when the temperature went down to two degrees.

I was finally bedded for the night. I discovered that my room-mates were five Sudanese ladies, whose husbands were billeted in the communal men's room, and the two Dutch girls. It was not a very big room and it was not insulated against the cold. The walls missed meeting the overhang of the roof by about two feet: an open gap remained at the top. My bed was at the back of the room in front of a wooden door which failed to connect with the door frame at the top, the bottom, and one side, and had great gaping cracks through the middle of it to boot. I discovered that for this accommodation I was going to be charged the enormous sum of six pounds, which was less than one Australian dollar. When quoting the price, the manager had seemed hesitant, as though he thought I might complain that this was surely the price for the whole room, not for an extra bed. I wasn't about to protest.

I wandered around the hotel and found that it was merely a collection of mud-brick huts built around a series of courtyards enclosed within a wall. At the front was a big hut with a large courtyard. This was the men's accommodation. The women's quarters were a row of smaller huts in front of a courtyard. The bare, packed-earth courtyards were swept clean, which seemed unusual after Egypt, but there was nothing growing nor any ornamentation. There was no electricity except for a generator, which came on spasmodically at night. It was the only one in the town; everyone else used lamps.

It had taken the whole afternoon to accomplish the bed and now, at five, I discovered that I should have by law registered with the police in order to spend the night in the town. I was too late. The police hut was shut. I was an illegal immigrant, but long past worrying about such details.

My thoughts turned to the possibility of a wash. I felt very grotty, as I had not had a shower since Aswan. I was disappointed in this too. Water was very scarce and hot water impossible. I doubt if any could have been found in the whole of Wadi Halfa. The women's ablution block was freezing, and contained only toilets, three of them in a row in a tin shed. They were the usual squat, hole-in-the-floor jobs, incredibly smelly and yucky, but a great deal better than those of the boat, for here there was no water to slosh around and make matters worse. The washing facilities were three taps in a row in the open courtyard, exposed to all. Only one tap produced a few drops of water. I gave the washing business a miss, and did a dry clean job with some cold cream and tissues.

I found the Dutch girls back in my room. We sat on our precious beds – I sat on Achmed's – and they told me how they came to be in Sudan. They had been employed as UNESCO volunteers, and had spent four months working for the government planning organisation in a town in western Sudan. They were a bright pair of girls who had enjoyed the experience.

Evening crept on us while we were talking and I felt the cold seeping into the room. Now the Sudanese ladies who belonged to the beds I had been stuck between returned, and, instead of expressing horror that their living space had been drastically reduced – there were now only thirty centimetres separating our beds – they were delighted and made a big fuss of welcoming me. Anywhere else in the world returning to your hotel room and finding a stranger shoved into your midst, practically sleeping on top of you, would be tantrum material. But these ladies were sweetness itself.

I was grateful for the little Arabic I had, because almost no one so far spoke any English. The Sudanese people I met were extremely generous and wanted to give me things, which worried me because they were so poor. They wanted to share their food with me, when I knew that they probably did not have enough for themselves. All I could do, to avoid giving offence, was take very little and give them something of mine.

16 Foul

It was now dark, so I went to the restaurant to see what might be offering. I had no high hopes. In a country constantly besieged by famine – and at this time Sudan was in the grip of a terribly bad one – it would have been gross to eat more than the one meal a day that the locals had, if they were lucky. The last time I ate seemed an eternity ago. It had been at eight that morning on the ship and the meal had been merely the last of my bananas and crackers. It was now half past six, and I was ravenous.

I sat down at the table of the other foreign travellers, who had also mustered for feeding time. They seemed to have commandeered permanent rights to a table which had become the unofficial Foreigners' Club, composed of members of that species who drifted up on the train, or down on the boat, and met briefly in this lonely place.

I went through the adventure of ordering food, having already had a practice run on buying cups of tea for the whole table. This cost only twenty cents but took about an hour. First I had to buy tokens from the cashier, who sat at a small table with a stack of tokens before him, then pass these through a hole in the wall separating the dining area from the kitchen. The hole was large enough to accommodate a head, a couple of hands, and a plate. I peered through it into a tin-walled lean-to attached to the back of the restaurant. On its earthen floor I saw a double-sided tripod stand containing hot coals, above which two enormous iron kettles were suspended. Two young Sudanese gents were in charge of the kettles and were busy making large quantities of tea, pouring it into sleazy glasses, after 'washing' them in a bucket of extraordinarily grubby water. I'd drunk a lot of tea already, and wished I hadn't seen this sight.

To obtain food the hungry hopeful paid twelve cents to the cashier, received a small piece of paper with something written in Arabic, and took it to yet another hole in the wall. I looked through this into another lean-to, where the cooking fire burned in a circular pit in the floor. A large pan on tripod legs stood over the fire. It was bubbling and steaming with the day's eats. I thought it very primitive until I saw the food, and then I realised it was sufficient unto the needs. Everyone got the same, and it turned out to be beans. I received my ration in a shallow, battered tin dish similar to the one our dog ate off at home.

The beans are called *foul* and, good grief, that's exactly what they were. They are the local staple diet. They taste like sawdust. To tell the truth, I haven't eaten a lot of sawdust, but this is what it must taste like. *Foul* are large brown beans with very thick outer skins that resisted all my efforts to chew. If the bean was like sawdust, then the skin was like woodshavings, and had the texture of them too. It was obviously expected that I eat skins and all, so I manfully forced them down with swallows of tea. *Foul* came floating in oil and, to add a very exotic touch, you could garnish them with a spoonful of the local crumbly goat cheese that came in an accompanying small bowl. The meal tasted absolutely ghastly, but for twelve hours I had had no sustenance except several cups of noxiously sweet tea. So I ate the lot, oil, cheese, and all. No utensils were provided, but of course I was carrying my own spoon.

The Korean boys had by now started to do their own cooking on the floor alongside the table, using a clean, shiny aluminium tray, a tiny spirit burner, and two cooking pots: one for meat and vegetables and the other for rice. They cut up the ingredients on the tray and in next to no time their meal was bubbling away on the floor. Imagine doing this in a restaurant in the west – what tolerance the Sudanese have.

When the meal was ready they offered some to everyone at the table. I thought it would be awful to take their food and had anyway started on the beans. The others said that the food was delicious and that the Koreans had been equally hospitable the previous night. They must have brought their own supplies with them, because I didn't see anything like real food in Wadi Halfa.

The Koreans, being Muslim, had won scholarships to study at Medina University and had taken up the offer of a free education. Saudi Arabia does much to sponsor other Muslims in this way, and gives a great many grants to Islamic men in countries around the world. The boys had travelled by boat from Jeddah to Port Sudan, from there to Khartoum, and were now going up to Cairo and on to Suez to make their way back to Jeddah by sea. They were, like everyone else, waiting.

The other foreigners and I sat in the restaurant talking until about nine. After a while it became apparent that we were providing the night's entertainment for what seemed to be the entire male population of the town, or as large a number of them as could squeeze into this shed. They must all repair to this haunt in the evening. What else was there to do? We were not doing anything spectacular, but we did provide them the chance to look at women other than their wives. It would not be possible to sit and look at Sudanese women in public. I never saw any women on the street in Wadi Halfa. In fact, I saw no local women at all. I suppose the odd female tourist who came this way was fair game, not that we were anything in the way of attractive specimens to look at, being unwashed, with untidy hair full of dust and sand. I felt horribly scruffy. The backpackers looked worse. They had more ingrained dirt than I did, and did not even try to look presentable.

Even in my unappetising state I had managed to garner additional proposals of marriage and, from a more sophisticated type, a quite charming proposition. Only the really basic souls wanted me for all time; this man merely wanted a lend of my charms. Given my appearance, you'd have to question his taste. My admirer was the cashier from whom I kept buying tokens for the ubiquitous cups of tea. He decided eventually, on the strength of our acquaintance, to open negotiations by saying, 'You have nowhere to sleep.'

'Yes, I now have somewhere to sleep,' I replied.

'No, you do not have a bed. I will give you a bed. You come home with me and I will give you my bed.'

'No thank you very much. It is very kind of you, but I could not do that.'

'Oh,' he said, hurt, 'you don't want to come home with me and sleep in my bed.'

'No thank you very much,' I said.

On a shelf near the cashier's desk was an old jam tin in which a few hot coals were kept burning as a cigarette lighter. Every man and boy I saw smoked. This made me sad. It is really pathetic to see people so malnourished and so poor spending their money on cigarettes. This almost universal addiction to nicotine is the result of the tobacco companies pushing cheap cigarettes and tobacco into the Third World in an effort to get everyone hooked. They see their chances of maintaining the *status quo* in the western world lessening all the time, and shamelessly concentrate on these other markets.

Just after nine – I don't know whether it was to get rid of us, or to fumigate the place – the manager put a few great chunks of incense into the hot coals of the jam tin, producing a pall of smoke: the whole place was fogged out in minutes. Someone said it was to cover the smell of *bangar* – although marijuana was frowned on, it was very easy to obtain in Wadi Halfa. I saw a couple of local men who were obviously stoned out of their minds, away with the pixies, with dreamy smiles and glazed eyes. There is no alcohol. Sudan is a Muslim state governed by the rules of the *sharia*, or holy law, and therefore 'dry', so they use what is to hand, and that is marijuana.

The light went out as the generator shut down for the night and the Dutch girls and I felt the way to our room, where we found the Sudanese ladies already asleep. I took to my bed unwashed and wearing all the clothes I could find, topped with my *abeya*. My supply of warm clothes was limited. It had not occurred to me that I would be cold in Africa and I hadn't needed woollies in Saudi. I had no covering except the grotty sheet. The wind blew directly in on me from all sides, the bed was uncomfortable and I dozed only fitfully, freezing through the interminable night.

At dawn the call to prayer sounded, and the Sudanese ladies got up to pray in front of the door. They wandered outside. One must have noticed that I was shivering. She came over and, without a word, covered me with her blanket, tucking me up as tenderly as she would have her own child. I was so moved I could have cried. But I was finally warm enough to relax and I fell asleep at last, ending one of the longest nights of my life.

Two hours later, I crawled out to face the task of getting myself on the train, which left that night. I had survived the night feeling that I had a gigantic hangover – I think I was affected by whatever had been thrown into the jam tin the previous night. I tried to clean myself a little, but without water it was impossible to combat all the dust and dirt I had accumulated over the past few days. I felt and looked exactly as though I had spent the night on a sagging cast-iron bed with a one-inch thick uncovered mattress without bed clothes, in a dirt-floored, mud-brick hut with seven other women and no electricity or water.

17 Two breakfasts to none

My first priority was to get a ticket for the train. I decided to do so before having a cup of tea – there being no more chance of food until the next evening's cook-up – and thought it would take me half an hour or so. I trudged through the sand to the building that had been labelled Tourist Office by someone in a moment of jest. It was a tin shed with a large space for a door, but no door, and spaces for windows, but no windows.

There was no warmth in the sun, it was still bone-chilling cold, and the shed was icy and empty. I had waited alone, for at least half an hour, when my friend, the alleged tourist agent, came past and saw me. He wore a thin *galabaya* and his teeth were chattering so much that he could barely speak. Like almost everyone I saw in Sudan he was painfully thin, with no fat to keep him warm. When I left I gave him my only jumper, hoping I would not need it where I was going.

He said, 'I shall take you to the ticket man to get your train ticket,' and frogmarched me up the hill to the railway station. This was another collection of mud huts, without platforms or other refinements. We were told that the ticket man had gone to breakfast, and so we waited for an hour until my friend suddenly said, 'There he is. You go with him,' then jumped up and dashed away.

I accosted the ticket man, who said (I think), 'Follow

me,' and set off at a scorching pace across the desert sands. I could not keep up as I plodded along behind. The sun had come out full force; I was still wearing my warmest clothes, covered by my *abeya*, and was becoming hot.

I had covered my face with my black scarf, not only because it was cooler, but because it prevented me from receiving, or indeed giving, unwelcome stares. I was aware that Sudanese people believe in the evil eye, and that I might frighten someone into the unnecessary expense of a visit to the witch doctor to neutralise the look I had given them. It was as though I became invisible the moment I dropped my scarf over my face; a peculiar, but safe, feeling. Islamic men never stare at veiled women.

By now I was feeling rather queer from lack of food. I had lost the ticket man, so I gave up and went back to the office where I had started. My friend was there again sitting on the sand in the sun outside the door, looking warm at last. I said to him, 'I lost the ticket man.'

He replied, 'Oh well, he has gone for his breakfast now, so you should wait here.'

I thought, peeved, that this man had had two breakfasts so far to my none, but wondered if perhaps I was translating 'breakfast' wrongly. I waited for another hour, sitting there feeling dreadful, until eventually I said I thought I should go to see somebody else.

He did not agree but said, 'Oh no, no, we will go again and see him.'

Back we went again to the station, but there was no one in the ticket office. I was this time taken into what was referred to as 'the head-master's room' – I presume they meant the station master – and given a seat. Another half hour went by. A young man came along and chatted to me very nicely, practising his English. After a while he produced an accomplice, and they proceeded to write my name in a book. Goody! I thought, this looks like progress. But I discovered afterwards that everyone will tell you that you have a seat, and everybody will write your name in a book, and twenty different people will give you a seat number, but there actually are no seats. They will sell most people a ticket but it will not have a seat number. The ticket comes with the understanding that it does not guarantee you a seat, merely the right to get on the train. In the lucky event that you do get a seat number, it will already have three people allocated to it. The train has seating for about two hundred but literally thousands will try to get on.

At half past twelve my stomach gave out. Malnutrition was setting in. I said that I must go and have a cup of tea and left, promising to return at one. My friend, who apparently had decided he was not doing any good, handed me over to another young man, who took me to what he described as the 'big' travel agency.

I had seen this place before. It had had something written on the door which looked hopeful, so I had tried to get in, but the door had been locked. (The other 'tourist office' had no door at all – this one's was permanently locked.) My latest friend told me that the agent locks it from the inside and you have to bang on the door for admission; hardly the way to gather a roaring trade.

The big travel agent's place was all very posh. Although it was only a shed like the little travel agent's, it had corrugated iron walls up to eye level and chicken wire the rest of the way to the roof. It had a wooden-framed door and a flywire enclosure like a verandah all around it. I went to the door and knocked. It opened and, lo and behold, there were six men sitting in this, to all outward appearances, abandoned place. Inside there was lino on the floor and even a desk – very lavish for Wadi Halfa.

One of the men spoke reasonable English, was much older than the others, and seemed to have authority. He said. 'Yes, yes. Well, the thing to do is for me to talk to my friend. I will do this. You come back in half an hour.'

When I returned he said, 'Yes, yes, I have spoken to my friend. Yes, he can get you a seat. What do you want? There is first class. There is second class. There are sleeping cars. There is third class. And then there's the roof – that's free.' Much as I like a bargain (and no matter how you look at it, free is the best bargain you can get) the disadvantages of riding free outweighed its bargain value. Countless people die from falling off the roof of this train.

The big travel agent said that inside the train it was necessary to pay for some class or other whether it came with a seat or not. For instance, you could buy a first-class ticket but still not get a seat; you might have to travel sitting or standing in the first-class corridor or lavatory. The cost of this privilege was the same as for a seat. The man also said that if I went next Sunday (it was now Wednesday) there was a possibility of a sleeper. (I shuddered at the thought of four more nights in W.H.)

Only a couple of compartments are actually used as sleepers. They have two bunks and only two tickets to these bunks are sold and they can be reserved. The difficulty is that they are permanently reserved for certain businessmen who go up and down all the time; no doubt *bakhsheesh* changes hands regularly to see it stays this way.

I said that I would love a sleeper, and the big travel agent continued, 'Only problem is we do not have ladies who travel alone, so the only spare one is with a man and, of course, that is *mamnoor.*' The way he said it was not a statement but a question.

'Yes,' I answered firmly, ' it is *mamnoor.*'

Mamnoor means forbidden, but I discovered that it does not mean as forbidden in Sudan as in Saudi Arabia, where *mamnoor* means 'totally and utterly forget it!' Here it seemed to mean 'if you want to go around it you can.' But with all the propositions and proposals I'd had so far I really did not fancy being locked up for several days and nights on a train with a gent who might think I had consented to cohabiting with him in the full sense of the word.

The big agent then decided that a seat in first class would be the thing. He said that I would be travelling with many other people, but vowed that I would actually get a seat to myself. I told him that I had heard of many people being sold tickets but no seats. He repeated that I would get a seat. 'Yes, yes, yes,' he said. So once more I was taken up to see the 'head-master' who, after a lengthy discussion with the big agent, took me along to see, with my very own eyes, the seat I would have on the train. I trudged behind him all the way down the desert sands along the long line of the train, climbed into the carriage and, sure enough, there under his hand, was the actual seat I would occupy. By now I was Doubting Thomas, however, so I asked, 'And how many other people on this seat?' '*Malesh*' ('No worries'), he replied, 'only six.' I asked him if he was sure there would be only six, and was content when he confirmed it. Only a few days earlier I would have fallen down laughing at the very idea and said I wanted the whole seat to myself, but now I knew that six was pretty good.

I said, 'Only six?' And he again promised, 'Six and only six.' He said he would write 'only six' on the door, and write the names of the six there as well to avoid any mistake. So be it. I felt sure that this was another fairy story, but he did it. I knew the crowd would not take much notice of it but, for what it was worth, it was done. I watched my name and those of five others go on the door, and then went back to the office, paid fifty-six pounds (about five dollars for a thousand miles) and was given my priceless ticket, a piece of tatty paper with hand-written Arabic scrawled on it. In response to my enquiry about the length of the journey, he said, 'It is two days and two nights when it doesn't break down and then it is a little longer, *en shal'lah*.' Great! I thanked him a thousand times, wished peace on his house, and departed.

All this had taken until two, and I was beginning to feel frayed. I'd had little sleep or food for days. I returned to my room, packed my bag, donned my *abeya*, and went out in search of provisions for the train. I found the local *souk*, a small open-air market not far behind the hotel, but there was little on offer. Apart from the iniquitous *foul* beans, all I could buy were a few bananas and some bottled water. There were no canned drinks or food. No problem. I could live on bananas and water, if necessary, for days.

At three I said goodbye to the foreign club at the hotel, who were all still waiting to be allowed to board the boat, and set off to take possession of my seat on the train. The Sudanese ladies gave me a present of a bright red, flowery hair ornament. I took a friendly farewell of the hotel staff after paying my enormous bill of one dollar.

The train was supposed to leave at five, but folk had been amassing, waiting to stake their claim in it, since morning. I intended to install myself in that precious, hard-won seat of mine. No one could push me off if I was sitting on it. Well, not easily. From what I had heard, however, it seemed likely that someone would sit on top of me.

I had seen no trace of a motor vehicle since I'd

arrived. I could only assume that the geriatrics had been returned to their mothballs for rest and recuperation until the boat returned to call on their services. I needed some means of getting my baggage down to the train, so I hired a donkey and its owner to escort me there. The man loaded The Monster on the donkey's back and off we set, he leading the little animal and I, wrapped and veiled, umbrella aloft as a sun-shade, ploughing along behind in the sand. An Arabian *memsahib*.

18 Six and only six

Sudan is the largest country in Africa, stretching from the Libyan and Nubian deserts of the north to the tropical rain forests and swamps of the south. The White and Blue Niles flow into the south of the country from Ethiopia, join together in Khartoum and then flow north through Egypt as the mighty Nile.

This was the country I had entered at Wadi Halfa and of which I hoped to see more, by courtesy of the train. The railway through the desert from Wadi Halfa to Khartoum had been built in the 1890s by British Major General Herbert Kitchener, who had been sent out to suppress the 'dervishes' who, fifteen years earlier, had conquered Khartoum and stuck General Gordon's head on a pole at the gate to greet the relieving forces.

My train had been standing in the station since before I arrived, so I'd had plenty of time to get a good look at it. The kindest thing to say is that it was an historic item. The Sudanese are still using the trains imported by the British, and they don't seem to have been repaired or maintained since the British went home more than forty years ago. They are down to their bare bones, almost derelict, and everything removable has been stripped off and sold. There is no water aboard, no heating and of course no air-conditioning – apart from the windows, from which the glass has been removed. They carry no food, even though they are notoriously slow and subject to long delays. The Wadi Halfa–Khartoum journey takes anything from forty-eight to seventy-two hours or more, depending on breakdowns and how long the train stops at the stations in the Nubian desert along the way.

I remembered the Australian consul in Cairo warning me that people took one look at this train and hightailed it home again. I hadn't really disbelieved him, although I knew that I for one would not turn back. Once I saw the train, I didn't doubt that others had. The thought of standing in a smelly corridor for two or three days, encased in a solid block of humanity, was daunting. I was the only westerner to board the train. I didn't see the Finnish threesome again after they left the boat; perhaps they returned to Aswan. The two German backpackers did, which surprised me because they looked rugged and seemed to have done a lot of hard travel. Soon after they arrived in Wadi Halfa the woman had burst into tears and refused to go any further. She'd said she was afraid of the country and afraid of the people, and once she had seen the train she knew she couldn't go on.

I had qualms, but was not going to retreat. It is not in my nature to go back when it is at all possible to go forward.

The train was very long, with an elderly diesel engine pulling more than twenty carriages and goods trucks over tracks laid on desert sand, as yellow and fine as that on a tropical beach, which stretched all the way to Khartoum. The carriage windows, lacking the touch of glass, allowed the elements free entry, so before long everything became covered with sand, including the passengers.

The carriages were built from tatty corrugated iron painted, long ago, a grotty shade of mustard-yellow, which matched the sand. Several thousand passengers managed to squash into these carriages, with five hundred riding 'unofficial class' on the roof. Many died each year after falling asleep and rolling off, and I was amazed that anyone could sleep perched on the rattling roof of a moving train. They must be relaxed people. I would have been clinging by my fingernails.

Official boarding of the train did not begin until three, but a mob of hopeful travellers had appeared long before this, and when the signal was given they rushed for the train. In my compartment I found that four Sudanese gentlemen in *galabayas* and turbans had already installed themselves, and another soon appeared. So far so good: we were the six authorised by the sign on the door – in a compartment designed for four.

We made our *salaams* and settled down to await departure. Two of the men were older than the others and looked distinguished. Intricate tribal scars, like the manhood scars of some Australian people, ornamented their faces. Decoration in the form of scars is found on Arabs and Africans, both men and women. Each tribe's scars are different and all have different meanings. The two older Sudanese seemed to have authority, because they were able to repel all the many attempted invasions by men wanting to share our home. When the train departed we were still only six, but I counted nineteen people in the compartment next door to ours.

The Sudanese gentlemen told me that, when it was time to sleep, I could have one of the upper bunks to myself. The men would sleep two men in each of the two lower bunks and one in the remaining top bunk opposite me. Obviously the men were then going to be very cramped, and I said I'd take as much of their baggage on my bunk as would fit. The luggage was overflowing the floor.

The train, amazingly, left around the scheduled time

of five, and rattled along steadily enough until the middle of the night, when its good behaviour ended with a monstrous bang. We shook as though about to jump the rails, and only the baggage jammed around me preserved me from pitching nose-first to the floor. The train stopped for a long time, with a great deal of shouting and confusion, and it transpired that one carriage had collapsed, probably due to the weight of passengers. It was a mercy that it did not drag the whole train off the rails. The five hundred or so people travelling in it blithely hopped onto the surviving carriages, dispersing themselves wherever they could. We took in two more men, who were obviously friends or clan of the distinguished gents.

The effect of this influx on the rest of the train was incredible. It seemed impossible that people could travel on for another two days standing virtually on each others heads, but they did, and cheerfully. I thought about the roof-travellers who must have been thrown off, but we heard nothing about them.

My bunk became my home for the next three days. I rested up there, out of the way, where I could still see down out of the window, for most of the day as well as the night. I could only stretch my legs out by putting them on top of the luggage, but I was grateful for this comfort.

I got off for some exercise when we stopped at one of the few railway stations along the way, keeping a weather eye open for the others from my compartment. I didn't fancy being left behind to wait for the next train. The stations were clusters of small mud-brick, flat-roofed buildings (the roofs need no slope for rain to run off). Whenever the train stopped the locals offered the awful omnipresent tea; it became ever more unsavoury, served in less and less attractive drinking vessels, the further we travelled from the civilisation of Wadi Halfa, which I came to understand was pretty upmarket compared to the villages along the track. There was very little food available.

The villages consisted of single rows of six or seven circular mud-brick huts with peaked roofs of straw. They looked very small, as though they contained only one room. Each village was enclosed within a wall and sat on the sand unadorned, except that some had a few date palms and an odd bush or two, or perhaps an old wooden cart standing around. The people were simply, often poorly, dressed.

My travelling companions treated me with courtesy and kindness, which showed their generosity of spirit. I must have seemed to them an abandoned woman. Wandering around without even a female companion, I obviously had no one who cared about me enough to protect me. Probably I'd been disowned by my family long ago and no wonder, if I had persisted in such degenerate behaviour. They were wary of me at first, but I behaved discreetly until they felt safe enough to offer me some food. Then, as I smiled and said, 'Thank you, Allah be praised,' and did nothing to offend them, they decided I was harmless, though probably mad. They shared their food with me, brought me cups of tea and ignored the fact that I must be a fallen woman.

I was lucky in a way not to be travelling with women. They would have been sleeping on top of me, and many more would have crammed into the compartment. The gentlemen let me get on with reading and knitting, which intrigued them no end.

Towards the end of the first day we came to a railway junction called Abu Hamid, where I was able to buy bananas, oranges and Pepsi Colas, and share them with

121

my companions. It also had a toilet of sorts, which was an improvement on that of the train, insofar as it was stationary. It didn't have water for washing, so I stuck to dry cleaning with face cream and tissues. I won't even attempt to describe the toilets on the train, one to a carriage. If you can imagine the results of all those people enclosed for days on end, with no water at all, you'll get the picture.

Whenever I dismounted from the train I put my *abeya* over my clothes and scarf over my face as protection from the sun and the curious, and to hide the ravages of the dirt and heat. I covered my face at night to keep off the flying sand and keep out the light. My companions seemed to think I was acting from modesty, so I would not be gazed on while asleep. I did not disillusion them. They studiously avoided looking at, or speaking, to me when I retired into *purdah*. (But I could see them!)

There was a light in our compartment which worked spasmodically. When it was working, it was left on all night, as it wouldn't have been seemly to turn it off while I was sleeping. When it was not working in the evenings we sat in the dark and the men spoke quietly to each other in soft, musical Arabic, which always sounded to me as though they were reciting poetry. Perhaps they were.

19 Elephant's trunk

It was pitch dark and very late on the fourth night when we finally reached Khartoum. By this time I felt as though I had been on the train forever. The engine pulled up a long way from the platform, and there were no porters. I was forced to manoeuvre The Monster outside to the street under my own steam, pushing it on its wheels with a little help from other travellers, who all had to struggle with loads of their own luggage.

I found a taxi and asked the driver to take me to a good hotel. He took me to a place in the heart of town called the Araak, with an impressive façade and a grand lobby, but mediocre rooms in which only half the facilities worked. It turned out to be a 'good' hotel in price but not fact. It was the most expensive I had yet stayed in during my travels, being one hundred dollars a night, payable only in foreign currency – horror! At that moment I longed for a bath so badly I didn't care how much it cost me. I was starving, but all they could offer me this late was a cup of tea with lemon. It cost ten Sudanese pounds! I felt guilty drinking it, knowing that although this was only about a dollar, it was more than most people here earned in a week.

I had a heavenly shower, even though it was merely a trickle of not quite warm water in a sleazy bathroom. To

123

be clean all over at once, hair and all, was divine. I had last washed in Aswan, over a week before.

I slept like a log and exited the hotel as quickly as possible next day. I bought a map in the shop foyer, and went to check out the lay of the land. I found better digs, a much cheaper lodging place, in a hotel called the Acropole. It was not far from the main street of town and served simple set evening meals, included in the price of the room, at a communal dining table. The food was adequate but monotonous, but I was pleased to get any food with the drastic famine ravaging the country.

The hotel was run by a Greek named George, an all-round good fellow who did much to help foreigners working or travelling in Sudan. His hotel was the unofficial meeting place for expatriates, journalists and relief agency workers, most of whom had their mail sent there. Cheaper hotels are usually run by Greeks or Sudanese, as opposed to the Egyptian or western managers of places like the Hilton or Araak.

Shortly after I left Sudan, the Acropole was bombed by terrorists and almost completely destroyed. Many people died. I felt sick when I heard this news. The Australian consul in Cairo, who prophesied my doom had almost been proved correct. I wondered if he was right then frantically digging out the letter I had signed exempting him from blame.

I spent the rest of my first day in Khartoum at the Aliens Office and the police station. I had to register my person at both of these places within twenty-four hours of arrival. This exercise left me many pounds poorer and took a few years off my life. Passing along a seemingly endless line of officials, filling out untold forms, and being called an alien did nothing for me. I had always pictured aliens as little green men wearing goldfish bowls on their heads. I was told that for each other town I wanted to visit a permit was necessary. As a permit took seven days to obtain, and was only valid for one town at a time, progress in Sudan would be very slow. My plans of further Sudanese travel began to pall.

Next day I sent my unsavoury train clothes off to the laundry – they almost walked by themselves – and, map in hand, went about photographing everything in sight, blissfully ignorant that it is forbidden to take photos without a permit.

The fabled name of Khartoum reminded me of history lessons in primary school and stories from childhood books. I should have come then; now it was too late. There is not much fabulous left. The anticipation I had felt travelling here faded into sadness at the sight of the all-pervading poverty.

Today Sudan is a Muslim state governed by the holy law of *sharia*, instituted after the British left forty years ago and independence was attained. The people of the south, who practise a mixture of Christianity, animistic religions and black magic, refuse to accept this law that bans dancing, eating pork and drinking alcohol. The result has been the war, between Muslim and non-Muslim, that has crippled the country. Sudan is also beleaguered by economic problems, drought, famine and disease. There are drastic shortages of medicine, doctors and nurses, and huge refugee camps, where more than half a million people subsist. Hundreds of thousands, half of them children, have died of starvation.

In the Acropole I met relief agency workers and journalists from all over the world. The reporters had come to cover the famine and report on the refugees fleeing the war in the south. They wrote about 'women with dry breasts feeding children with match stick legs and men reduced to skeletons sitting by at camps'.

Khartoum is built where the Blue and White Niles meet, on a piece of land between them resembling an elephant's trunk, or *khartoum*. The towns of Omduran, North Khartoum and Khartoum combine to make up a city with a total population of nearly five million. In the streets of Khartoum town, which were laid out by the British in the shape of the Union Jack, I walked under arcades and shady trees past colonial buildings. In the wide main street, once the centre of a prosperous slave trade, there was little activity. The few vehicles on the road were predominantly Land Rovers, Toyota utilities and ancient battered buses and trucks almost as derelict as my former transport in Wadi Halfa.

I found few consumer goods in the shops, and most of them were very dear. There were, however, traditional Sudanese weapons such as swords, daggers and knives, and quantities of local silver and ivory jewellery. Ebony and ivory carvings were cheap; but ebony is too heavy for plane travel and ivory is prohibited. I bought a copy of an ancient Egyptian scarab beetle charm, carved in turquoise-coloured stone and set in silver.

One evening George from the Acropole found me a taxi to cross the river to Omduran to see its *souk*. The taxi was a beat-up old Toyota which did not possess a meter – par for the course here – and a lengthy battle of wits ensued before the driver and I arrived at an acceptable fare. It was far more acceptable to him than to me, however, as he had an unfair advantage. There were no handles on my side of the doors.

Handing over my ransom money, I extricated myself from his rusting heap and clambered out to find myself in old Islam, which came as quite a shock after the British colonial of Khartoum town. Omduran was built by followers of the Madhi – a nineteenth-century Muslim leader who had been defeated by British General Kitchener in one of the last set piece battles of the British Empire – and retains its Islamic style and atmosphere. It has small streets and its mud-brick buildings and houses are mostly flat-roofed and single-storeyed. It was more like a huge village: goats, donkeys and camels wandered the narrow streets and crooked alleys. Here and there the thin minaret of a mosque, or an occasional palm tree, rose above the low buildings. I had no trouble finding the *souk*, Sudan's biggest market, which it dominates the scene. Moving into its depths I discovered an enormous array of local goods, but little food. There were stalls and shops selling ebony, ivory, gold and silver. But there was not the vitality and exuberance found in Egypt's Khan el Kalilli, nor the variety of goods.

On this side of the river the streets were crowded with people, mostly men, and everyone I saw was, as in Khartoum town, dressed conservatively. Men wore *galabayas* and the loosely wrapped turbans called *emmas*, and women wore *thobes*: several metres of coloured material wrapped about the torso and head over a long gown. Some women were veiled. I saw a few men in western dress, but no women. I was told that less clothing is worn in the non-Muslim south; in fact, some people wear nothing at all.

The local restaurants I visited in Khartoum town used the same token system of payment that I had mastered in Wadi Halfa and didn't supply eating implements. I learned to use bread to scoop up food and shovel it into my mouth. This is not a bad method of ingesting a meal, although I usually made a dreadful mess. Fortunately, washing water was always provided before and after. Food was simple, with few spices. Most dishes are flavoured only with lemon, salt and pepper. Apart from the mainstay of the diabolical *foul*, with which I had already engaged in mortal combat and had no wish to meet again, there were pita bread; salads of tomatoes, lettuce, onions and capsicum; *sgerifa*, which is like spinach; *addis*, a yellow lentil, often served in broth or oil; fish in the form of Nile perch; and lamb kebabs. The only dessert I was ever offered was a dish of chopped bananas, figs and raisins, which was delicious. Tea, called *shai*, was served sweet, with mint, cinnamon or cloves. Coffee was Turkish, thick and strong. I liked the fruit juices sometimes available, in particular *kakaday*, made from hibiscus flowers, and *limoon*, lemonade and guava. There was Pepsi, but no Coke. I presumed this was for the same reason it is not allowed in Saudi – they say the Coca-Cola company is Jewish-owned.

Only one or two of the major roads were paved in Khartoum. As soon as I rounded the corner of the main street, heading for my hotel, I was in a dirt road littered with rubbish and lined by tumbledown mud-brick houses. I was told not to walk at night, only during the day. The few times I ventured out alone after dark I did so very carefully in the middle of the empty, unlit street, tripping over stones and rubbish. It was hairy. I had my feet ready to break into a canter at the first sign of trouble.

I went to the Hilton hotel one day for lunch and met an American engineer who was working in Khartoum. We were just getting on the outside of a good meal, when gun-shots exploded close by. Someone had tried to assassinate a visiting Asian head of state as he went out the hotel's front door. I didn't go back. I should have known better than to go there in the first place. I always try to keep away from this sort of place in volatile countries, where ritzy hotels harbour people who invite bombs. Even the Acropole, which no person of magnitude would have set foot in, turned out to be a target.

I found another lunching place instead; an old colonial hotel in a shady tree-lined street by the riverside in North Khartoum. The dining room was a cool, dim cavern, a haven of wood-panelled walls, vast ceilings and softly whirring fans. I sat alone in solitary splendour, with three waiters to myself, and ate lamb kebabs.

I investigated all means of travelling onwards, and found that there was no plausible way to continue except to fly to Nairobi in Kenya. Land travel was not permitted through the war-torn south. Even flying over this area could be dangerous: planes had to dodge missiles flung at them by resentful rebels. Buying a ticket was not easy and extremely expensive. It cost just a little less to fly to Nairobi than to buy a return ticket to London. I had hoped to travel south down the Nile by steamer, but this method of travel had been banned for foreigners because rebels were shooting at ships (and occasionally hitting them, too). An article in the local paper at this time was headlined, 'Steamers hit'. The story was about rebels attacking a convoy of steamers making their way down the Nile, and sinking two. It was possible for intrepid travellers to journey east through the country on market lorries, as long as they were prepared to withstand the dust and sandstorms. I had thought about going east to Port Sudan, the only port on Sudan's coastline on the Red Sea, to see if I could get a ship from there, but the Koreans I met in Wadi Halfa told me this was a dreary, boring place.

To buy a plane ticket I had to produce receipts for the travel agent to show the government that I had changed money officially to pay for it, as well as a civil aviation permit, an exit visa, and a visa for Kenya. The latter necessitated more passport photos. I went to a local studio and was photographed carefully by an earnest young man. Glowing with pride, he presented me with the results. 'You are very beautiful,' he enthused. I did not destroy his fantasy, but I thought they looked like the mug shots of an axe murderer.

The choice of airline was easy. It was either Sudan Airways, otherwise known in this region as *En shal'lah* (God willing) Airways, or Kenyan Air, with whom I flew. The travel agent paid a large bribe on my behalf for someone to waive the regulations and allow me to use unofficial cash to buy my ticket.

I took a taxi four and a half kilometres to the airport. As the plane rose above Khartoum we passed over the confluence of the two Niles. From this height, they both looked blue, cutting their broad channels through the dry, brown earth.

Flying over the south was nerve-wracking. Rebels had boasted that they had ground-to-air missiles capable of bringing down planes, which was a good reason for not flying by the government airline, quite apart from its Third-World status. I noticed a few passengers looking decidedly fidgety besides myself.

On the plane I met a young Irish registered nurse, Maureen, who had been working as a volunteer in a remote village in western Sudan. She was going on leave to Kenya to meet her boyfriend, a medical student who had flown from Ireland to join her. She was taking full advantage of the sudden availability of booze after a long dry spell in Sudan, and I joined her. I had, after all, been in there more than two weeks myself. As in Saudi Arabia, even arriving in Sudan inebriated or in possession of alcohol brings instant arrest. We became friends and decided to go together to find a hotel in Nairobi.

20 Female circumcision

Maureen told me about her work and life in a village in Sudan, about living in a mud hut with a straw roof and dirt floor, and the primitive conditions and intense heat she worked in with her sole helper, another nurse. She also told me about female circumcision – the barbaric mutilation practised almost universally in Sudan – and the problems arising from it that she saw in her work. I had been aware of this custom – it is practised by a minority of Saudi Arabians – but I had no idea how prevalent it was elsewhere, or of its horrible effects and its great death toll, until I read a book on the subject that I chanced upon in Khartoum on the small shelf of English-language books for sale in the Acropole hotel. It was written by a Sudanese woman doctor, herself circumcised as a child, who had undertaken a study of the practice, hoping to lead the way to its eradication. This will be hard work as the subject is taboo and cannot be openly discussed.

Maureen confirmed what I had read. She told me that the operation is done when the little girl is between five and eight. Several people are needed to hold the child down. All the tissue inside the labia majora is excised and the labia are stitched together with only a small opening left. Afterwards the child's legs are tied together for fifteen to forty days.

The awful operation is most often performed by ignorant people in unsterile conditions. Sixty per cent of the operators are grubby, untrained old women, who use no anaesthetics or antibiotics. They use razor blades, locally-made steel knives, sharp stones or scissors. Even trained midwife operators sometimes use an old bed covered with a dirty rag and neglect to wash the area first, using one unsterile needle for everything. But educated and enlightened parents, as well as peasants, subject their much-loved female children to this unspeakable cruelty. (And I never saw people who loved their children more than the Sudanese.)

In her clinic Maureen had treated little girls suffering from the immediate complications; shock, haemorrhage, fever, difficulty in passing urine, and urinary infections. Many children died, especially those who were not brought to some kind of medical help. If the child survives the ordeal, at the age of eighteen or so there is even worse to come. On her wedding night, there is another trial: the scar tissue must now be penetrated by the groom. The risk, apart from pain and terror, is of haemorrhage and infection, the same as from the initial operation. Consummation of the marriage can take up to eighteen months of distress, but a man who seeks help is not regarded as a real man. Husbands resort to razor blades, a friend to hold the wife down, even acid, to open the scar tissue. It is considered normal for the woman to tear, bleed and suffer severe pain. Childbirth brings further risk of rupture, haemorrhage and damage to the baby's head.

It is an unbelievable fact that, after giving birth, most women return voluntarily to be recircumcised. The social pressures on them to do so are so great, they may even be divorced if they do not. A man has the right to divorce his wife for any reason he chooses.

Why is this mutilation done? It is firstly to satisfy the fragile male ego that the bride has been touched by no man before. Secondly, it is supposed to give the man (no one gives a thought to the woman) more pleasure if the entry is exceptionally tight. The first claim is farcical, for circumcision actually facilitates the covering up of a previous defloration – all the errant girl has to do is get restitched. (If it is at all possible to err in a society which guards its women so closely.) As for the second claim, what a peculiar definition of 'pleasure', inflicting the agony of trying to penetrate an entrance which has been reduced to the size of a pencil or less and is guarded by thick scarring into the bargain. The only way is to actually tear and rend the tissues. Some pleasure!

It is widely, but incorrectly, believed to be written in the Koran that women should be circumcised. But not only religious beliefs influence the practice; social factors are also involved. In the south where the people are not Arab, nor influenced by Islamic customs, circumcision is not universal, but it is still practised. In northern and central Sudan, which are predominantly Arab, ninety-nine per cent of women, whether Muslim, Christian or animistic, are circumcised. The few girls who are not circumcised come mainly from parents of higher education. But the fact remains that most girls will not get a husband unless they are circumcised.

Here is a description of a circumcision, written by one of the operators. 'I hold the external genitalia, from the junction of the two labia, in my left hand, and the knife in my right. I cut the tissue from its roots and continue downwards, then I pass my hand over it. If I find any more tissue I will excise that too totally. Next I put some dough from *merissa* (a locally fermented alcoholic drink) or animal excreta on the wound and press down very hard until the bleeding stops. Then the legs are bound together as usual. Healing may take up to fifteen days. Then you can feel just a skin over that area without any flesh, this is why it is called *Tahara dalokia* – like a drum.'

21 Picha la cowboy

The plane landed at Nairobi after a two-thousand-kilo-metre flight in the late afternoon, and we were met by sunshine. Nairobi is only a short distance from the equator, but it sits high above sea level in the fertile highlands, and its climate is mild. The Jomo Kenyatta international airport was a let-down, a sterile modern place, with no African personality at all, except for the people. Kenyans are mostly tall and solidly built and generally have rich-brown skins. The Sudanese are thinner and much darker, verging on black at times.

The people of Kenya are made up mainly of numerous indigenous tribes, a large number of whom live in their traditional manner, and of whom the Kikuya are domi-nant. There are also the descendants of Arab merchants, slave traders, and the 32,000 Indian labourers who were imported in the 1890s to build a railway across the country from the coast to Uganda. A small, wealthy minority of Asians, Arabs and Indians now own and manage hotels and businesses. Britons and Europeans began to settle in Kenya from the turn of the century. They numbered about 80,000 by the time the Mau Mau began the push for independence in the 1950s. By the time the Mau movement fizzled out in 1956, its recruits, who were made to swear blood oaths to kill Europeans and their African collaborators, had despatched 13,500 Africans and one hundred whites. During this reign of terror many white Kenyans left for good and now only half a per cent of the present population is of European descent. Independence was finally won in 1963 and Jomo Kenyatta, 'The Lion of Kenya', was the first president.

An airport minibus was available to travel the ten kilometres to the town, so Maureen and I availed ourselves of it rather than take on the rugby scrum waiting at the taxi line, where passengers were pounced on by drivers touting their attractions and mentally doubling their prices at the sight of any innocent-looking lambs.

The hotel we chose was on the outskirts of the city, where the wealthier citizenry lived. From the window of my room I looked down into a neighbouring private garden, a haven of green bushes and tall trees splashed with the vivid colours of bougainvillea, frangipani and hibiscus. I needed this after the desert. The music of birds woke me each morning (after which I rolled over and went back to sleep like any right-minded person would).

I settled in and adjourned to the restaurant, which doubled as a bar. It took up most of the front of the hotel and was, I suspect, its chief source of income. It was heavily patronised during the evening and night. Some of the female patrons looked suspiciously like Flowers of the Night, and they seemed to be doing a roaring trade. The food was good and cheap and, as an obvious tourist, no one bothered me except a very old African man trying to sell a carving. I watched two obnoxious American men, who obviously had no intention of buying his carving, making loud, rude fun of him. He took this with a confused smile on his wrinkled face. He approached me timidly, and I bought the awful thing. Just what I needed, a heavy carved wooden statue! How would I explain my way through Australian customs with it? It sits watching me now as I write; I've actually grown quite fond of it.

I was joined after a while by Maureen and met Patrick, who had arrived the night before. We spent a long time in the bar while Maureen caught up on her alcohol consumption (she was true Irish, very fond of beer), and I got in some solid eating. Then, well stoked up with life's bounty, we went off to the casino for a spot of gambling.

The next morning, after a late rising and a good brunch in the bar, we set off across town with an obliging taxi driver who, for a commission, delivered us to a black marketeer and negotiated some money for us. Black market money wasn't easy to acquire and, judging by the fuss surrounding the getting of it, carried an element of risk. The exchange rate was officially sixteen Kenyan shillings (one hundred cents to a shilling) to the Australian dollar, but much more could be obtained on the black market. We had had to fill out currency forms on arrival in the country and were supposed to account for our money when we left but, once again, as in Sudan, no one ever asked for my form. The original Kenyan currency was beads and cowrie shells; one hundred shells to one blue bead. The first East African postage stamps were typed by Ugandan missionaries and had values of five or ten cowrie shells.

Proceeding to the tourist bureau, I bought a map and we set about exploring the sights. We went to the shopping streets where, to my delight, I found a Woolworths' supermarket. It was wonderful to be let loose on masses of edibles after my recent deprivations. I went mad buying goodies in packets, boxes and jars: all essential supplies of course. The merchandise did not run to anything exotic, but fresh fruit was wonderful, abundant and cheap, as were the grains and other local produce I bought to make my muesli. Pineapples cost about twenty Australian cents each and were sweet and delicious. Passionfruit were eighty cents a kilo – that's a lot of passionfruit!

Most of the goods in the shops seemed extremely old-fashioned. Cosmetics and make-up all looked as though they had survived from the 1940s. Sadly, items such as skin-lighteners and hair-straighteners did a big trade. There was usually not much problem being understood. The shopkeepers spoke English or Swahili. Swahili is a marriage of Bantu, Arabic, English and words of many countries, and has evolved into a common language from the need to communicate and trade. It contains some lovely English assimilations such as *kiplefti* – a street sign – and *picha la cowboy* – a western film.

That afternoon the Irish contingent and I paid two hundred shillings apiece for the privilege of clambering aboard a city tour bus and being trundled around like a herd of sheep. This excursion took in the Snake Park, which I could have managed without, but I loved the humorous signs. 'Trespassers will be poisoned', and, by the crocodile pit, 'Those throwing litter into this pit will be required to retrieve it'. There were two hundred species of snakes and reptiles, including tortoises, crocodiles and turtles. Some of the venomous snakes were housed in open pits and others in glass cages. I would have preferred them left in the bush where, with any luck, I would not have to gaze upon them. In one large room were the non-venomous snakes. At feeding time they are fed live frogs, which is quite horrible – especially for the frogs.

After lunch we went to the National Museum and saw displays of natural history – stuffed animals and birds, elephant tusks, ethnic tools and weapons. There was a complete room of paintings by Joy Adamson (the woman of *Born Free* fame) and a case full of religious, magical and medical items: sandals soaked in donkey urine to be used for prophesying; magic sticks, made from aluminium tea kettles, with which to talk to God; spells for rain making; charms of horn, shell and bone to be worn for protection; amulets in the shape of genitals, used by women to promote conception; and cursing objects, which can be used by anyone.

Fetishism, black magic and the main religions of Christianity, Islam, Hinduism and paganism all manage to get along together peaceably in Kenya. In fact, they are intermingled. Polygamy, for example, is widely practised, even by Christians.

Next on the agenda was the Railway Museum – a joy for train buffs – with old carriages and steam engines lovingly restored and maintained. The *pièce de résistance* was the inspection coach from which Charles Ryall, a British railway inspector, was snatched from his bunk by a lion and eaten.

22 The call of the wild

Kenya has long been famous for safaris, and it still has the most wild animals of all the countries in East Africa. I had always wanted to try a safari – probably as a result of a misspent childhood at the pictures on Saturday afternoons with Tarzan – and Patrick and Maureen were of like mind. Our problem was choosing among the hordes of touts who besieged us in the streets, all quoting different rates and modes of travel and accommodation. Only after much harassment did we choose a fellow who looked slightly more harmless than the rest. We went with him to his firm's office, pursued by a trail of rejectees all moaning that we had chosen badly and prophesying doom. We would be stranded in the desert, robbed, raped, pillaged, and eaten by wild animals. They were bad losers.

The expedition we chose lasted five days and the price included food and accommodation, which consisted of tents. This seemed a good offer, though it was hard to tell what you might find once you set off. The real touristy safaris, costing mega-bucks, offer lodges, surrounded by stockades, where viewing is arranged. The animals come by appointment to drink or eat under lights. It sounds very comfortable, but is not like seeing animals in their natural state. I was told that many of the lodge managers are retired big game hunters. How tame this must seem to them.

The cheaper safaris, like the one we chose, involve camping out, erecting your own tent and helping with the chores and cooking. They offered either cold showers or none at all and were for people who could 'do without comfort in order to gain an unforgettable experience'. They promised to be more like the authentic safaris (except you don't kill anything) – no dust-free, air-conditioned vehicles or planes and luxury lodges with hot water. Having served my apprenticeship in rough travel on the Wadi Halfa trail, I didn't want to do things the cushy way.

It was agreed that the tour driver would pick us up at our hotel the day after next at seven in the morning – shudders! All this arranging and paying took a long time and it was quite late when it was concluded, so we returned to our hotel and settled down to more eating.

Most of the food at the hotel was simple European cooking, which was a relief. From what I had read about African cuisine, it sounded plain, to say the least. Bananas and *ugali* – maize – are staples, as are tasteless dishes of millet, sorghum, beans and cassava root. Fried flying ants are a delicacy. Local drinks are cheap and interesting, if you don't value your life too dearly. There is *pombe* – as in bomb – an African-style ale made from bananas; or *malwa*, made from millet or honey in the manner of mead. Western-style beer is brewed locally, as are wines made from fruit, roots, and a lot of pot-luck. A powerful palm wine toddy, *tembo*, is for the adventurous only. If that doesn't finish you off, there are locally made gins and brandy, which vary from batch to batch. To rehydrate, you can tempt fate with the water, which is sometimes safe to drink. A sign in one hotel proclaimed, 'All the water in this establishment has been passed by the manager.'

The following day we went to the railway station (the Irish team had decided to keep travelling in my company) and bought tickets for the night train to Mombasa, departing on the evening we returned from the safari. I had decided to go to the coast and try for a ship rather than travel overland any further. After paying for our first-class sleepers, we were told that the price did not include bedding. For the privilege of covering our bunks with a sheet, and ourselves with a blanket belonging to the Kenyan Railways, we were required to cough up another twenty-five shillings – about one and a half dollars. That evening we paid the hotel the balance of our accounts – they had required a hefty deposit up front when we booked in, which confirmed my opinion that they were used to short term tenants – and asked the receptionist to store our suitcases until we returned. Then I packed a small overnight bag. For once I was travelling light, because the safari tour company refused to allow anyone to travel with more than one small bag. I bid The Monster a reluctant farewell.

I arose at dawn the next day snarling and complaining, but was ready and waiting long before the minibus arrived. It was late. Our safari was going to the Masai Mara, biggest of the wildlife parks of Kenya, being 1800 square kilometres of dry-grassed plains and small hills. It has more animals than the other parks and is the best one for game viewing. About four hundred kilometres from Nairobi and almost a full day's travel, much of it over unmade roads and difficult conditions, Masai Mara is in the far south of Kenya, and is a continuation of Tanzania's Serengeti National Park. Ernest Hemingway immortalised this area in his novel, *The Green Hills of Africa*, and short story, *The Snows of Kilimanjaro*.

The minibus was full. There were seven intrepid safarists

as well as the driver, who was also our guide and guard, and the cook. Guide and cook were both young Africans. Although we were collected early from our hotel, it was a couple of hours before we amassed the food, the cook, and all the equipment ready to leave. Finally we headed out from Nairobi on a main highway going south. Before long the road began to climb through low hills and we passed the turn-off to Karen, the former home of Baroness Karen Von Blixen, author of *Out of Africa*. We drove through villages of plain houses with thatched or tin roofs. The countryside and crops were more picturesque. There were acres of white pyrethrum daisies, grown for insecticide; grassy slopes; green woods; roadsides coloured with flame trees and Jacarandas; stands of banana trees; tea growing on gentle hillsides (Kenya grows one third of the world's tea); and coffee plantations.

On the other side of the escarpment the country became drier and wilder the further we went. We crossed the Seyabei River and stopped at Narok for a picnic, which we enjoyed under the shade of Jacaranda trees in blue blossom. This was the end of the bitumen road, which had been deteriorating steadily until it was merely a single strip of ruts and potholes. It was better, however, than what we were about to encounter.

About an hour after Narok we arrived at the Masai Mara Game Sanctuary barrier gate, from where it was a further 160 or more bone-shattering kilometres over rough and dusty tracks before we reached our camp site towards evening. At the gate I met close up my first Masai warrior. A bunch of them were hanging about leaning on their spears. Driving along we had seen an occasional one minding a herd, standing with one foot resting on the other knee to watch us pass. The warlike Masai, tall, proud and bloodthirsty, invaded from the north about

250 years ago. They are pastoralists who keep great herds of cattle and are feared and respected by other tribes. I can see why everyone is afraid of them. They are very aloof and superior-looking.

The guide and the cook seemed to know their way around and chose an open space of red dirt, surrounded by thick bushes and scrub, as our camp site. We were not segregated from the animals in any way; they were all around us, although none was visible. The guide had a large rifle. I hoped he knew how to use it, and wished I had one too. The rules forbad anyone from leaving their vehicle or walking anywhere except in the areas specified as camping places. There were community showers and toilets a couple of hundred metres away, but we were warned not to walk there or anywhere else at night. The cook told the story of the American lady tourist who ignored this warning. All that was ever found of her were her sneakers. (Indigestible?)

Around sundown we piled into the minibus and bumped away over rugged country to see the animals. The land reminded me of the plains around the Pilbara in Western Australia, especially in the glowing colours of sunset. The red earth was covered with grass and studded with trees, bush and dry scrub and now and then we dipped through a dry creek bed. The air was very clear, so you could see a long way into the distance.

The bus roof lifted up and we took turns, two by two, standing up to look out or take photos. Although I had seen these animals in zoos, I could not believe the difference it made to be with them in their natural habitat.

Most of the animals ignored us. We got quite close to a couple of tame-looking lion prides, lying on rocky prominences and playing with their cubs. They had become used to the sound of motor engines and seemed to accept the buses as some kind of animal that shared their living quarters. They didn't recognise the people inside as food – the bus's exhaust fumes disguised our smell – but we were told again that we were never to get out of the bus. I had visions of the bus becoming bogged, and being the one chosen to push it.

An old male elephant gave us a shock when he charged the bus and chased us away from his herd. Up close he was enormous, with huge, furiously flapping ears, and he was trumpeting fit to shake the earth. You cannot believe how large an elephant is until you eyeball one in the wild like this. Then you vamoose.

A leopard looked down on us from where he was draped elegantly along a tree branch. Vultures sat hunch-shouldered in dead trees, giving us the evil eye. Herds of wildebeest and warthogs – the essence of ugliness, round barrel bodies with ridiculous flag-like tails – ran past, as did zebras, gazelles and antelopes. They are food for the predators – lion, leopard, cheetah and wild dog – and scavengers like hyenas and vultures.

Rhinoceros lumbered crossly away from us like small armoured tanks: two tonnes of short-sighted bad temper that will charge at anything. Its horn is supposed to be an aphrodisiac, and so is illegally hunted, but I can't imagine how swallowing any part of such an unattractive item as a rhinoceros could enhance your sex appeal.

A giraffe paused in his evening meal as we approached and calmly raised his head to look at us. All we could see of him was a length or so of neck and a curious head sticking up over the treetop. We also saw many gazelles: the dainty *dik dik*, always found in pairs, and Thompson's gazelle, with its white flashing tail, as well as gnus, the animal clown, with their crazy cavorting.

They say that metre-long monitor lizards, 170 species

of snake, and crocodiles also live here in abundance, but I am happy to say we did not see any.

We came to a wide river fringed with green, in which groups of hippopotamuses, the river horse, sported ponderously. Weighing in at around two tonnes, hippos eat forty-five kilos of grass each night. They look deceptively placid, but can kill a lion and are fast enough on land to catch a man. Rivers and lakes should be avoided for another reason too. Apart from the crocodiles and hippos they contain an additional nasty, the minute snail that is the host of *bilharzia*, a particularly disagreeable parasitic disease. I resisted the urge to immerse myself in the inviting streams of Kenya for this reason, and kept on taking anti-malarials because, although malaria is not common in the highlands, it is on the coast and in the bush.

Back at the camp we ate our evening meal on logs around the fire, in front of the tents we had pitched before setting out to see the animals. My bright red tent was minuscule, a one-man job and a small man at that. I was grateful that the good-natured cook took pity on me, a mechanical illiterate – getting the lid off the jar of Vegemite is a major mechanical feat for me – and helped me put it up. (I actually had no trouble getting it up, getting it to stay up was the problem.)

We were well fed, considering the cook's equipment: three battered pots and two ancient frying pans. He was a happy young man, and did a fantastic job in the saucepan department.

During the night the sound of lions roaring, elephants trumpeting and wildebeest snorting came very close. Hyenas came right up to the tent, and several times I woke to see one silhouetted on my flimsy nylon wall. I could hear them snarling and crunching the bones that we had thrown into the bush. I had heard of men sleeping outside who had had their scalps ripped off by hyenas' powerful jaws. In Saudi I had once seen a Bedu with ghastly lacerations to his scalp caused by the wild dogs of the desert. There is something repulsive about the skulking hyena. When we were sitting outside, he would never approach, but would sidle beyond the edge of the firelight, waiting, a vague shadow just at the limit of vision.

At times during the night baboons made a fearful racket, hooting and calling while they fossicked among the bushes around us, looking for leftover goodies. The fire was kept going all night and I suppose the guard kept an eye on us: it would have been bad for business to have us eaten. One man summed up well the safari when he wrote: 'The experience of having that which one would normally only see on the other side of cage bars, actually with only a piece of canvas between one and them, was unforgettable.' I quite agree. I managed to get to sleep, but some of the others didn't.

We were awakened at dawn and bundled into the bus for our morning ride out. It was still not quite light, and off in the distance we could see two multi-coloured hot-air balloons rising slowly, materialising above the plain like space ships. We assumed that the tourists in the balloons came from the expensive lodges behind the stockade fences, for ballooning was a costly exercise, that included a champagne breakfast. I imagine drifting close above the animals must be a great experience – but what if you are forced to land unexpectedly? For the animals, manna from heaven.

After breakfast we walked over to the rough camp bar, and spent a couple of hours drinking beer and playing cards. By afternoon the baboons in the bushes grew bolder. The minute a tent flap was left unguarded, they zipped inside to seek dietary supplements. One large female, with tiny baby firmly attached to her front, was particularly persistent. I chased her out of my tent and she took off clutching a large box of tissues. She turned around to face me and casually flipped out tissues one by one, scattering them to the four winds, as though she had been doing this all her life. Those tissues were invaluable to me as toilet paper, serviettes and face washers as well as nose blowers. I salvaged what I could.

The park covered an enormous area. Over the next four days we seemed never to pass through the same spot. Our clothes, hair and persons became dirty from the dust. The showers didn't always have water and, when they did, it was only a trickle of brown brackish stuff. But we all looked as scruffy as each other so no one minded.

It was boiling in the middle of the day and we sought refuge in the camp bar, where I found a few local newspapers. I realised then that there were greater dangers in Kenya than those posed by rhinos or baboons. One paper reported on the inquest into the death of a man who had been shot in the thigh with a poisoned arrow. The judge concluded that no one could be held responsible, as the person who fired the arrow was at the time guarding his maize plantation from wild animals. Another told of animal rustlers who shot dead a man and his wife on their farm, broke into their grass hut and made off with four goats. Three gangsters armed with sub-machine guns had ambushed a motorist in the main town, taken the car and left him by the side of the road. A sixteen-year-old, pregnant girl from the Rift Valley had bled to death after her circumcision ruptured during labour. Female circumcision has been forbidden in Kenya since 1982, but it still takes place in rural areas, and is accompanied by frequent deaths.

We survived the safari, arriving back in Nairobi in the early evening just in time to collect our luggage and board the night train to Mombasa. In my tradition of always keeping in good with those in charge of the eats department, I farewelled the cook and gave him a substantial tip in appreciation of a job well done.

We set off in the train through the gathering dark. Villages, people and the odd wild animal presented themselves for our inspection at the windows as we journeyed past. The train was straight from colonial days: wood-panelled walls, brass fittings, old-fashioned wall-bracket lights with shades, and a dining car with white-jacketed waiters and starched damask tablecloths and napkins. Whenever the train stopped, women with trays and baskets on their heads offered us fruit, fried ants and other delights. Night trains run, very slowly, in both directions daily, taking around thirteen hours depending on the number of cattle, wild animals and tribespeople wandering on the line. Although slow, trains are far safer than taking to the road in a bus, the drivers of which, like Egypt's, are all frustrated *grand prix* entrants.

My compartment had two berths, a wash basin which pulled out of a 1930's wooden cabinet, drinking water in a glass carafe, a wardrobe, a fan, and the twenty-five-shilling-extra bedding. At the press of a brass bell a liveried attendant popped up like a genie and took your drinks order. After a good night's sleep between clean white sheets – oh, memories of the Wadi Halfa train! – and a pleasant breakfast, there we were, moving through the bustling crowds on the Mombasa platform.

23 The Great Ship Search

Mombasa is a port of legend, evoking ships, sailing, and adventure itself. In this world of aeroplanes, if I still had a chance to travel by sea, surely it would be from here.

We climbed down from the train and stepped into colour, noise and activity. I was aware immediately of the difference between Mombasa and the rest of Kenya. It has a unique character created by the mixture of its many cultures. The first recorded mention of Mombasa dates from the twelfth century, when it was described by Arab travellers as the home of the King of the *Zenj* – Arabic for 'black Africans'. By the time the Portuguese arrived in the sixteenth century, Mombasa was a well-known port and trading centre that shipped ivory, skins and slaves to Arabia. Over the centuries, Indian, Arab, Asian and European traders settled here, and towards the end of the nineteenth century the British, in an effort to suppress the slave trade, established a colony.

Maureen, Patrick and I decided to indulge ourselves for a few days and stay at the best hotel, the posh beachside Oceanic, which incorporates Mombasa's casino and looks out over scattered suburban houses surrounded by high, grim fences. I was given a largish room on the second floor, with a stunning view of the channel between island and mainland. That evening the casino downstairs lured me in for the night, and I contributed generously to the owners' pension fund.

I was blasted out of bed at first light by a great horn that sounded like the trumpet-call heralding the end of the world. I stumbled to the window, drew my curtains, and reeled at the looming apparition of a huge ship, apparently about to enter the room with me. That was how I discovered that the channel outside was the way all shipping came and went, usually in the early morning, to the port of Kilindini. Wonderful. I watched, fascinated, as a long procession of boats glided majestically by. Among all these ships in East Africa's largest port, surely there must be one for me.

Downtown Mombasa was very quiet. An election was being held, and this had provided the excuse for a public holiday. The two Irish bods and I walked up and down the wide main street, every now and then being hustled by street sellers and black marketeers, who called to Maureen and me, 'Jambo Mama' ('Hello, Missus'). We discovered that both ends of the main street led to the sea. Mombasa is built on a small coral island that is connected to the mainland by a causeway.

The weather was sticky, which was not surprising seeing we were standing virtually on the equator. In the past this area was known as the White Man's Grave, because deaths from endemic diseases such as malaria were common. To escape the heat we found a restaurant and, for a nominal fee, had a two-hour lunch. The prices fell dramatically away from the expensive hotels. In the small supermarket we bought supplies to restock our emergency rations, which I had vowed never again to be without after Wadi Halfa. A bottle of local gin, labelled Gilbeys by someone with a sense of fun and no qualms about copyright infringement, cost five dollars, but a book in English, second-hand, battered and with a trade-in, cost three. Perhaps they recognised my need.

Two days later I moved into a hotel in the town, the better to pursue a ship. Also, although the Oceanic was not high-priced by Australian standards, it was too expensive when travelling for an indefinite time with a fixed number of traveller's cheques. I usually try to live somewhere near the level of the local cost of living when I am in a place for any time. Hotels at which people of the country or expatriate workers stay are always more interesting than those stocked with tourists.

This hotel was called the Splendid, which it was anything but. It was, however, cheap and right in the centre of town. It seemed to have a lot of visitors who stayed very briefly, and on the floor below me was a massage parlour. I peeped into this one day to see a lot of garish red lights and decorations and some most friendly girls who called to me, 'Hello, hello. Come in.' I declined gracefully.

Upstairs on the rooftop was a beer garden, complete with umbrellas, and a restaurant which I patronised solidly. The food was plentiful but not thrilling: potato and curry, or rice with curry, fish and chips (common on menus here – a legacy of the Poms) and mixed grills. Swahili food, which I tried in local restaurants, used a lot of coconut and coconut milk. I loved the fresh fruit juices. Passionfruit and pineapple juice were served hot in the evenings and were even more delicious that way. There was even an ice-cream parlour close to the main street. I sampled gingerly at first, but typhoid didn't strike me down.

The roof-top area of the Splendid seemed to be a pick-up joint, but no one bothered me. I'm not to everyone's taste. When Patrick, Maureen and I were together we discovered that the locals thought we were both his wives. Poor Patrick: a fate worse than death. When alone I ate and drank and minded my own business. Only once did an African man follow me down the stairs, saying, 'I shall come with you.' I said, 'No thank you, I am going to meet my husband.' He didn't persist.

Booking into the Splendid required a sizeable deposit, an indication of the usual clientele. Imagine my surprise when I entered the hotel reception to the sound of Slim Dusty wailing that the pub had no beer. They should have played that at the Kaki in Saudi.

I set seriously about the Great Ship Search. I didn't particularly care where the ship was going, except that it should be heading in the general direction of home. I could worry about the rest of the journey later.

From the local paper and my phone calls to shipping agents, it seemed that ships there were a-plenty, but none that carried passengers, except a couple that took cargo and a few passengers regularly to South Africa. My feelings for the policies of that country (in those days) precluded my visiting it; well, safely, anyway.

Undaunted, I set off on the rounds of the travel agents. They all said the same thing. There was no way I would find a ship. No passenger ships had called here regularly for years. The fabulous *Queen Elizabeth II* was going to stop here on one of her round-the-world cruises and, yes, there were spare cabins as far as Australia, but they cost the price of a small house. I decided I would rather have the small house.

Next I went personally to all the agents and explained what I wanted, saying that I did not mind a cargo boat and was able to do with minimal comforts. I finally spied a glimmer of hope. A travel agent directed me to a large shipping firm, where I was eventually washed up at the desk of the seemingly boss person, an African man of massive proportions and serious charm. He studied me intently, trying to decide whether I was batty. I must have passed – whether that meant he thought I was, or wasn't batty, I can only wonder – because at last he said he would endeavour to help me. He said he would try to find a suitable cargo boat captain. Through this kind man, Mr Tauni, I eventually secured a ship out of Mombasa.

In the meantime, I learned to use the local transport, which apart from buses are *matutas*, vans which you wave at madly until they screech to a halt. The driver gives you only enough time to insert part of your body before taking off again in a puff of smoke. To get out of the *matuta*'s intestines you shout, 'Oi!' or something equally uncouth, whereupon you are jettisoned, with luck still retaining all your bits and pieces as you pick yourself out of the gutter. I finally got the hang of them, meantime travelling to a lot of places I never intended to go. By this means, and on foot, I explored the town and surrounding areas.

The shops were stacked with tourist items, as Mombasa is on the package tour itinerary from the UK. Some shops had clothes, but the western fashions were very unattractive and old-fashioned. The colourful *kangas*, a one piece wrap-around Swahili garment that most East African women wear, were very pretty.

Beggars filled the streets, as they had in Nairobi. I selected one for my own and contributed to him daily. When I had my first encounter with beggars, years ago when I went to work in Hong Kong, I was terribly distressed and did not know what to do. A Chinese friend told me to give to one regularly and that one would protect me from the pestering of the others. I have noticed that most westerners cannot cope with beggars; even though they donate to them they cannot look them in the eye. That must be the worst affront, to be treated as though you are not a real person. This particular beggar in Mombasa had no legs or arms. He was only a torso and head, but had bright, lively eyes and a smile which illuminated his face whenever I spoke to him.

A week later I moved to a better and even cheaper hotel, a place I had found in the main street called the New Palm Tree. It had a palm tree all right, but if ever tree or hotel was new, it was a long time ago. The rooms were upstairs on two floors, and faced a large central courtyard with a potted garden containing the afore-mentioned palm tree and his brethren.

A sign in my room advised me that, if I wanted to have tea, the room boy would heat water for me in his 'electric cattle'. Wow! A switched on cow.

I sat outside in the courtyard at night with a drink and met the other guests. One young woman was a newly graduated English doctor doing a three-month elective at the Mombasa hospital. Her revelations about the treatment and local lack of understanding of AIDS were alarming. She quoted statistics and said that the authorities either ignored or denied them, not wanting to jeopardise their tourist industry. She said that Kenya, already known as the home of AIDS, had at least one in four people with positive antibodies.

24 Standing in a line and jumping up and down

Maureen and Patrick had moved to a coastal resort on the mainland at Likona, where they were staying in a beachfront chalet. They told me a horror story over lunch one day.

They had come back from breakfast that morning and had sat on the edge of the bed to write a postcard. Maureen had dropped her pen and, as Patrick had leaned down to pick it up, he had noticed a pair of boots sticking out from under the bed. He had got down on his knees and seen that the boots were attached to a set of legs, which in turn were joined to a long, lean body lying flat out, as stiff as a board, under the bed. Patrick, who was a fine big broth of a boy, dragged the body out. The long lean person said that he was drunk and didn't know where he was, but it was plain that he had come to steal. Patrick and Maureen let him go, but told the management and the house boys caught him in the bush. No doubt they dealt with him in their own way. As compensation for their trauma Maureen and Patrick had been moved to an upmarket unit at no extra charge.

I had been warned often, by Kenyans themselves, that thieves were rife in their country. Not long after Maureen and Patrick's experience I saw a robbery myself. I was waiting in a crowd at a bus station on Jomo Kenyatta Avenue. It was six in the evening and the working crowds were going home. I hadn't seen another white person all afternoon. A bus pulled in, causing a stampede. Bodies flooded over the street. Suddenly I became aware of a fight. I saw a young, jean-clad, red-singletted man with a firm grip on another thin and ragged man, who seemed to be struggling to get away. He suffered karate chops, kicks and a good bashing before he eventually broke loose. I felt sorry for him, and considered chasing after him to administer first aid. Then I saw a red purse lying on the ground. A young woman leaning from the open window in the bus gaped in amazement. It was hers. Someone passed it to her. She examined her bag, a big striped canvas carry-all, and held it up to display a large cut that had been slashed in it. The crowd chattered excitedly. The young hero was congratulated. I gawked with the rest of them, drawing the attention of the only policeman within miles. He flagged down a passing car and obviously said, 'Give this lady a lift away from here or I'll book you,' or words to that effect, for he got me a free ride to the GPO.

Another day I saw a man run over by a bus. (Well, his bike was.) He was pedalling through the intersection of Moi and Digo, the main streets, when a bus driver going around the corner failed to see him. The passengers shouted warnings from the open windows – luckily for him the buses don't have air-conditioning – and he just had time to fling himself, but not the bike, backwards to safety. There was a sickening crunch as the bike was mangled under the bus's wheels. The bus driver tried to get off the bike by reversing, which only mutilated it more. The man, who had fallen to the ground, got up, apparently unhurt. He was a poor-looking Indian wearing a *dhoti* and turban. He stood leaning on the corner railing with his head in his hands. I guessed that the bike was a huge loss to him, but at least he was alive. A young African woman shouted what sounded like abuse at him out of the window of the bus. A large crowd gathered in a flash, but the bus, relinquishing responsibility, moved off. I wanted to go up to the man and say, 'I am sorry,' but I didn't. No one did. I regret that still. If he had been hurt, the nurse in me would have gone immediately to comfort him, but the onlooker stood aside with all the others.

Downstairs at the New Palm Tree was the obligatory bar, always well frequented, and a large dining room that reminded me of staff dining rooms in Australian country hospitals. Here at lunch one day I met Tom, who was a retired American, and an amiable, intelligent and good man. He had made a lot of money in business and had come to Mombasa to ask the leaders of his church how he could use his money to help the poor. Every now and then I meet someone like this, who restores my faith in humanity. We became friends, went out together for meals, and he introduced me to many people.

After two weeks Maureen and Patrick left by train for Nairobi, from where it was to be Sudan again for Maureen and Ireland and medical school for Patrick. We hugged and kissed on the platform, knowing we'd never see each other again. Ships in the night. A few days later Tom also caught the night train to Nairobi. I saw a lot of the station over these few days.

I met Rani Khan, the owner of a travel company. He was the answer to a maiden's prayers: tall, dark and handsome, with flashing Indian eyes. He took me to dinner at a fancy restaurant on Bamburi beach and then we raged on at the Bora Bora night club, which featured a floor show consisting of drums and wild African dancing. I learned to do one of the local dances, which consisted mainly of standing in a line and jumping up and down, both of which I'm pretty good at. But I think I'll stick to the tango for romance.

One day Rani had business to do in Malindi, up the coast, and I went with him. We drove for an hour or more through stretches of grassland, palm trees and sisal plantations until we came to the Kilifi Creek crossing. Here we had to get out of the car to wait for the ferry. An enterprising vendor came along offering coconuts, which he beheaded with one slash of his machete. We continued on, passing through villages to a chorus of 'Jambo' from the children playing under kapok and jack-fruit trees, until we came across the turn-off to 'Africa's Ankor Wat', the Gede ruins.

These are the remains of a mysterious pre-Portuguese Arab-Swahili town of about 2,500 people, abandoned in the sixteenth century. The ruins are hemmed in by dense jungle covering more than nineteen hectares, an easy place to get lost in. Rani and I walked through the undergrowth under huge boab trees, listening to bird calls and scurrying animals. I could understand why no one stays after dusk in this spooky jungle cavern. I felt the presence of spirits, and they weren't on my breath.

Rani took my hand and we clambered over the remains of a palace and several mosques and single-storeyed houses, the sanitary systems of which were sophisticated enough to run to bidets. There were many large tombs scattered around, topped by great phallic pillars. The tombs indicate that the inhabitants weren't African, as the pagans disposed of their dearly departed by poking them up in trees, rather than burying them in boxes. The architecture at Gede is Arabic, but artefacts found there are from

India, Persia and China. In the caretaker's small hut were red-lacquered glass, eye pencils, shards of Chinese Ming dynasty blue-and-white and celadon porcelain, and thirteenth-century glass and glazed earthenware from Persia.

Rani went about his business at Malindi, and I went into the Blue Marlin hotel, where Hemingway drank the town dry, and set about lunch. The drinks list offered a 'Bloody Merry'. Too right, I thought. Verb or adjective, it would do me.

Malindi is not just a tourist town. It supports itself by fishing, growing crops and brewing palm toddy. Many up-country settlers retire or holiday here in fine houses. In 1589 the townspeople were in danger of being eaten by the Zimba, an all-male cannibal Bantu horde, who swept all before them by putting their enemies in the pot for food. They helped the Portuguese conquer Mombasa and then began eating their way up the coast. A neighbouring people saved Malindi by defeating the Zimba. (Perhaps they were more voracious eaters.)

Malindi's ancient records mention the Chinese traders who took slaves and ivory from along the coast, and chronicle the visits between 1417 and 1419 of the junks of the Chinese emperor, Cheng Ho. A giraffe, complete with an ambassador to feed it, was once sent to the emperor of China by the Sultan of Malindi.

Rani's business was finished at last, and we drove out to one of the beaches called Silversands, which it wasn't. It was, however, a place to sit quietly under a beach umbrella with a drink and watch the surf foam in from the sea. Eventually it was time to leave this idyll, and we stopped for dinner at a two-storeyed, lamp-lit restaurant, where the top floor overhung the beach. Later we sat on the upstairs verandah and listened to the waves murmur beneath. It was a special night. A perfect tropical evening, with the scent of flowers on the breeze; a dark, velvet night of no moon except the slim crescent belonging to the banner of Islam.

While waiting for my ship to come in, I went walking round Mombasa. I strolled down to the old port, where dozens of wooden *dhows* were moored, and sat on the wall to watch one as she wafted gracefully over the sea that Vasco da Gama had sailed on his search for India. An arched entrance here leads to the Thirty-Nine Steps. After British law banned slavery, slaves in irons – people of the inland and the mountains, who were terrified by the very sight of the sea – were secretly brought down these steps. A *dhow* or a *zarook*, the fleetest vessel to sail these waters, would glide in noiselessly after dark, collect the human freight, be away before dawn with the morning breeze and clear of the land before sunrise, heading for Arabia. If a patrol ship chased after the slave boats, and capture seemed imminent, the traders would drop their contraband black ivory into the depths. Arab slave traders raided inland from the coast of Kenya for centuries. It is said that slavers still operate off Zanzibar and along from Lamu, an island north of Mombasa, and that slavery will never die out in some of the Arab states.

25 Hello sailor!

Four weeks had passed since I had come to Mombasa. The Anglican Bishop of Mombasa, to whom my friend Tom had introduced me, invited me to lunch with his family. In the middle of lunch, Mr Tauni, the mountainous shipping agent, who had somehow tracked me down, rang with startling news. 'I have a captain coming in an hour. You must meet him.'

I leapt into action and rang for a taxi. It didn't turn up so, with the aid of the Bishop's wife, I took a bus into town. I rushed panting into Mr Tauni's office and found that he, admirable man, had managed to detain the ship's captain there. This Dutchman was tall, slim, blond and bearded. He looked squeaky-clean and handsome in his tropical uniform of white shorts, shirt and long white socks. He questioned me charmingly, but guardedly, in excellent English. He said that he would not normally take a stranger on his ship. Later he told me that he'd had to consider the possibility that I was involved in drug-smuggling or was a desperado on the run from the law. But, *al hum d'alah*, he agreed to give me passage to Bombay. He could have said the moon, I'd have been just as pleased. I felt as though I'd won the lottery.

Pieter was the name of this gorgeous seaman. He was the master and part-owner of a small Dutch cargo ship, the *Pandora*. She was a tramp ship, which doesn't mean that she was down at heel or loose with her affections, but that she was not tied to regular routes, and wandered wherever cargo could be collected or delivered. How romantic, I thought, the perfect life for a nomad like me, born with itchy feet and insatiable curiosity. (I have often wondered if I was exchanged by gypsies in the cradle, I am so unlike the rest of my tribe.)

I asked him the fare, and he told me that he was not legally permitted to carry passengers, and would have to put me on the manifesto as a crew member. I signed on eventually as the Ship's Nurse. For one dreadful moment I had thought he was going to ask me to cook, something I have always strenuously denied being able to do.

The *Pandora* was sailing next afternoon, so I dashed off to say goodbye to Rani and other friends, telephone home, stock up on munchies from the supermarket, give my beggar a golden handshake, collect my laundry, and buy some tatty books at astronomical prices. When the captain came to collect me, I was ready and waiting. He took me to Mr Tauni's office, said he had to attend to urgent business, and commissioned Mr Tauni to take me out to the ship.

We proceeded to the customs shed. Two stony-faced Kenyans asked me if I had any Kenyan money left and, having forgotten to get rid of it or hide it, I answered, 'Yes.' They said that I must return to the town and spend it. Poor Mr Tauni, looking as though his worst fears about my sanity had been confirmed, raced me back to the main street, where I rushed into the first shop to buy something. The charming Indian storekeeper greeted me warmly and, with a dazzling smile, assured me that what I needed was a 'genuine aquamarine stone with a written guarantee'. The smile and the greeting were not false, but the stone was. It turned out to be a genuine piece of glass. Serves me right. The shopkeeper went to wrap my purchase and I hid the rest of the money in my bra. I still have that ill-gotten loot. No one in all the world wants Kenyan money. Your mother was right: crime doesn't pay.

I still had the change the shopkeeper had given me; about four hundred shillings. I gave the big notes to Mr Tauni, telling him that I hoped he would not be offended, but I had to get rid of them somehow. He didn't seem too put out – he looked as though I could use him as a repository of all the unwanted money I liked. The small notes I gave to the customs men as a sign of goodwill. This influenced them not to search my bags, which was lucky, as they contained a prohibited bottle of gin.

Traumas over, Mr Tauni and I clambered into a tiny motor dingy. We putt-putted through the harbour, wending our way in and out of the multitudinous ships in the port, and I peered up at the massive hulls, wondering which was the *Pandora*. I was frightened by some derelict, rusting messes, but overjoyed when my boat loomed up in front of us, a wonderfully pretty ship, shining with fresh paint.

I climbed up a wobbly ladder as the crew hung over the side and watched the arrival of this eccentric woman who was to be their shipmate. My large and clunky luggage embarrassed me. The Monster seemed about to sink the ship. At last, after much perspiration, it and I were installed in a well-appointed cabin, with attached bathroom, on the top deck. I couldn't believe how I'd fallen on my feet. This must surely have been the best cargo ship on the coast, with the most respectable-looking crew.

26 Pandora

The *Pandora* sailed out of Mombasa harbour at ten at night on Wednesday 10 April, carrying 3500 tonnes of lentils and me. This spick and span tramp steamer of one hundred metres and four thousand tonnes had a crew of seven charming Dutch officers, two sailors – a Portuguese and a Sri Lankan – and a cook who was also Sri Lankan. The ship had experienced trouble with her engines, and had been laid up in harbour for days getting them fixed. While we were waiting for the pilot to take us out, we went a short distance to test them. We sailed slowly up the narrow channel and passed close by the Oceanic, the grand old hotel, standing majestically on the edge of the water.

We returned, took on the pilot, put ashore the two engineers who had been doing the repairs, and were finally away. By now it was a dark and glorious night. The wind had dropped to a mere breath and the sea was calm. The stars twinkled in the blue-black sky as we moved out into the Indian Ocean and made our way up the dark coast of Africa. Now and then a phosphorescent flash at the side of the ship marked the passage of a large fish.

I watched the last of the shore lights fade away, then slept like the dead until morning. I spent the next day in total idleness, enjoying the cool sea air, resting, and taking meals in the officers' mess, where we all ate together regardless of rank. This was a democratic vessel, where the sailors' own mess was not used. A delightful touch was that grace was always said before meals.

The officers and sailors were polite, nice-looking fellows. When I thought about the grotty ships and evil characters I had heard of, I realised that someone had taken care of me – either that benign providence that protects fools and innocents or, more likely, the excellent Mr Tauni. With the exception of the Sri Lankan men, they all spoke perfect English.

The cook, whose name was Santos, which means 'saintly' – a description I did not agree with; I privately named him 'The Great Race', because he was the slowest mover I have ever seen – was dour in the extreme. I only saw him smile twice: once when the ship was pitching in high seas and I went rocking and rolling along the deck past the galley, tripped, fell, crashed into the siderail and nearly went overboard as shark food; and another time, at the end of the voyage, when I gave him an American twenty dollar bill in pursuance of my policy of staying friends with the cook. Santos allowed no one to enter his galley and brooked no criticism of his culinary skills. The captain told me he had learned this from sad experience. Good sea cooks, I was told by the crew, are rare birds and no one would risk losing even a halfway decent one. At least Santos was sober, and he didn't try to hack up the crew with a cleaver, as former cooks had done on this ship. One had imbibed the entire contents of the bar in the first two days, gone into the DTs, and become so violent that he'd had to be confined to the brig until the ship had reached the next port. The captain had been forced to take over as cook as well as master on the bridge.

Pieter, the captain, was a dashing man of about forty.

He was the epitome of the Hollywood old-time sailing master, except for the shorts and socks which showed off his great legs. I always resent a man who has better legs than I, although it doesn't take much. The first mate was a younger and even more handsome edition of the captain and they, two of the engineers, and a couple of land-based gents in Holland, owned the ship. They took great care of their maritime home, which gleamed with love and attention.

My cabin's portholes allowed a panoramic view, and a fresh sea breeze wafted through when I opened them. There was even air-conditioning. This was no Wadi Halfa-on-water. Also on the top deck were the captain's cabin and his sitting-room and office, a comfortable room with a resident philodendron. It seemed to be quite happy at sea, having twined and curled its way halfway around the room.

At midday, well out by now on the lonely Indian Ocean, we sighted three whales – 'the great ones of the under sea', as Arab seafarers call them – two adults and a baby. They came close to us, sporting and blowing water high in the air with a loud whooshing noise. The clarity of the water made them look even more awesome: eighteen or twenty metres of living flesh, weighing over a hundred tonnes, only a few metres away.

In the evening we watched a video in the officers' mess. They only had a few, and we watched some of them several times before we got to Bombay. This night it was *The Great Race*, and it was after this that the cook got his new name. Another favourite was *The Blood in the Tomb of the Mummy*, which was every bit as bad as it sounds and true to title, with oodles of blood and gore and a script of absolute drivel. We loved it!

Suddenly we were galvanised by the clanging of the

alarm bell. The engines stopped. The crew disappeared immediately, and I was left alone with visions of life-boats and emergency rations – particularly emergency rations. I was trying to decide what to wear to a shipwreck, when the second engineer returned and said that we had burst a water pipe. It took two hours to fix. While we sat becalmed the sailors turned on a bright light on one side of the ship to attract fish. They appeared in bright multitudes. We caught some large squid, which the cook served to us next night for dinner.

I sat on the rail gazing into the depths, which the light made green and transparent, and watched the teeming life beneath us. The world I'd known seemed remote, as though it was now a thousand years ago and we were alone on this gently rocking ocean. It was a night for dreaming.

27 Mother's little helper

I felt guilty about hitching a free ride on the ship and tried several times to pay for my passage. Captain Pieter refused, but I – Mother's little helper – found ways to justify my position on the crew list. The second engineer had an ear infection, a nasty *otitis externa*, which I treated twice daily. The ship carried ample supplies of medicines and equipment. I syringed the captain's ears, which were impacted with wax, cut his hair and trimmed his beard. The crew packed up laughing, but the results were successful enough to encourage the rest of them to submit themselves to my services in the barbering department. They had been at sea for months around the coast of Africa, where the hairdressing establishments are only for the strong in spirit who don't much care what they look like. They were all, especially the sailors, wild and woolly around the skull regions, but I set to with a will and shore the lot, except the cook, who was far too grand to allow a loose foreign woman to take liberties with his person.

I became barmaid. Everyone assembled at the bar fifteen minutes before lunch at half past twelve for one beer, and at half past five for another before dinner at six. I became possessive about my bar and set about spring cleaning it: polishing the mirrors, the woodwork and all the pretty bottles, even defrosting and cleaning the fridge. Never being able to resist interfering with anyone's pot plants, I took over the care of the captain's philodendron, giving it a wash in milk and lots of chatting up. I did the washing and ironing and generally played den mother to all the crew, hoping that news of this would never leak back to Australia, where I had always made it known that such duties were not for me. I even did their mending! I sat for hours on the bridge repairing overalls (when I wasn't doing my knitting), keeping company whoever was on watch. The men said they got very lonely up there all on their own, with nothing to look at but sea and sky. I learned a lot about sailing and navigation and even how to read the ship's log, which the crew told me was towed behind the ship on a rope in the water. I was convinced that I could make a life of sailing. Even when the sea was rough, I loved it. I have never been sea-sick, even in terrible storms.

During the second night the ship stopped again at the ring of the alarm bell. No one came to tell me to man the lifeboats, so I went back to sleep. In the morning I learned that there had been a problem with the exhaust system. For quite a while we could only make nine knots, and the captain was growing anxious. We had a deadline to meet to collect the next cargo, and the lentils we were carrying were needed urgently to relieve a famine. He spoke with the ship's agent in Bombay by radio and was told that there was another cargo waiting for them in Colombo after Bombay. He invited me to continue on there with them. I was delighted. There was even a possibility that they would go on further east to Singapore, from where it is only a short hop to Perth. The rest of the crew agreed that I could sail on with them anywhere I wanted, as long as I continued to do their barbering.

The morning had dawned cool and calm, but as the day wore on a wind had sprung up from the north-east, head on and slowing our progress. Now it shifted around, and our speed picked up to ten knots, top speed for the *Pandora*. During the following night, a swell arose and the wind changed again to the north-west. It became hotter and visibility deteriorated because of a heavy haze in the atmosphere. Pieter explained that this was caused partly from sand blowing down from the *khamseen* of Saudi Arabia (good grief, that place was still haunting me!) and partly because the air temperature, which was twenty-seven degrees Celsius, was less than the sea's. He told me he did not like this kind of haze because it reduced his visibility to four kilometres and it took him five kilometres to stop the ship from this speed.

One day there was flotsam – pieces of wood and leaves – on the water coming out from the shores of India, sixty miles away. I saw a container lid with three big fish cruising along underneath using it as camouflage. We passed across the way of three huge oil tankers; one going to South East Asia and the other two in the other direction of the Arabian Gulf. I hoped they would escape the missiles of the Iraqis, who would no doubt be lying in wait for them.

Once again the alarm bell rang and we stopped. Not for long, but it was all lost time and our provisions were beginning to run low. The beer was already finished and the potato box was empty. Our estimated time of arrival was once again deferred. The morning, however, found us only two and a half hours off the coast of India. There was a cool breeze and the current was behind us, helping the ship make better time. The captain gave me the job of making the currency, watch and clock list, ready for customs in Bombay. Everyone began a spring clean ready for what they called The Black Watch – the customs search. Indian customs officials are apparently convinced that all cargo ships, especially little tramps like this one, are loaded to the gunwales with illicit wares: drugs, whisky, watches and clocks. Indian customs officials have a particular suspicion of watches and clocks and they make a big fuss about how many each person has.

With the coast in sight, but no beer to celebrate it, I made the supreme sacrifice and let the men each have a little from the bottle of gin I had bought, for emergency and medicinal purposes, from the wine shop in Mombasa. We ate a sparse lunch of bread and jam. The Dutch cut theirs up and ate it with a knife and fork as is, I believe, the custom in Holland. It was too slow for me.

Dinner time came as we slid among the fishing traps and boats that extend twelve miles out from the shore, and at dusk we came to the point where we were to meet the pilot. A message over the radio told us that the pilots were changing shifts and there would be a delay of two hours. We dropped anchor to wait and sat on deck watching the lights of the ships come on. The pilot arrived on time and conducted us into a stream anchorage among the fishing fleet.

We dropped anchor only a mile from the shore. It was beautiful here. The lights from the tall buildings on the land shone out over the dark water, while the lamps of the fishing fleet glittered like paper lanterns at a party. The only sounds were the creaking noises of *dhows* and other wooden boats. In the dark of the night I saw a fishing boat under sail suddenly take shape, gliding noiselessly out of the void and slipping effortlessly to her berth. I heard the splash as the anchor went overside, the rattle as the chain ran out, then silence.

By daylight the harbour looked bigger, but much of its beauty evaporated. Smog from the shore spoiled the visibility, and the water was a sleazy mud-coloured soup. But there was plenty to see. I counted fifty ships in our vicinity and watched the smog slowly lifting from the city in the morning light, and the coming and going of the small boats. A wooden Indian coastal trader with four sails drifted past and out to sea.

The Port Health Authority officials came aboard and cleared us to go alongside. The ship's agent came out in a motor boat and promised to bring back essential supplies. He told me that, as I might be leaving the ship here, I must make a list of all my belongings, such as watches, clocks (again!), jewellery and electrical items. I did this dutifully.

We spent the day waiting. The ship was silent, as though it too was waiting. After dinner, when we were watching *The Great Race* for the third time, two shadowy forms loomed up on the outside portholes. Hooray! It was the agent with food and beverage. Everyone stampeded outside, only to find, to our utter disgust, that he had brought only the price list. Curse the man for a complete fool! Did he think we cared about the prices, when we had starvation staring us in the face? I sympathised with the supposed recipients of the lentils; we too were being denied food by bureaucratic incompetence. Captain Pieter threatened to keelhaul him. In a desperate effort to drown our sorrows we resorted to emptying the dregs of all the bottles along the back of the bar, exotic liqueurs and the like, which up till now had been safe from our attentions. We made up a poisonous cocktail, enough for two thimblefuls each.

Another day of waiting followed, during which neither the agent, nor our docking orders, arrived. That night shadows went past the porthole again, and we rushed eagerly outside to find that, oh rapture, our supplies had arrived. They took an hour to offload, and turned out to be alcoholic 'essentials' but not food: the person sending the supplies obviously knew sailors well. I threw a case of local beer on ice and settled down to playing barmaid.

We decided to drink up and forget about our empty stomachs. We did this well, and by the time I rolled away and fell into bed I was feeling no pain. The person who stared at me from the mirror as I attempted to clean my teeth looked crosseyed, but contented.

Bad news arrived next morning. The contracts to Colombo and Singapore had fallen through, due to the delays getting to the wharf. But customs officials came aboard and, after an intense search, cleared the ship.

Finally that afternoon a rough little work-horse, gloriously misnamed the *Wenus Vatervays*, pulled alongside and offloaded our food stores. The male contingent of the crew were seduced by the Carlsberg beer that came with the food, but I abstained, having signed the pledge that morning.

I did not have a visa for India. I hadn't had time to get one in Mombasa, and I was told I could get one without any trouble on arrival. The ship's agent had taken my passport and was supposed to be organising this for me, but I was rapidly losing faith in his abilities. He hadn't even done too well at feeding us. He also said he was trying to get me ashore. If I had had a visa I could have hitched a ride in with any passing boat. As crew, I was only entitled to a shore pass, and you have to be officially at the wharf to receive one.

At last, after six days of waiting, came the great news that we were to go alongside at six that evening. This was soon amended to six the next morning, but hope of a Singapore cargo was revived when the agent radioed from shore with an offer from a company wanting machinery delivered. I kept my fingers crossed. I had become fond of my floating home and adopted family. At three in the morning I awoke to the noise of the anchor being raised and the engines starting. Praise be to Allah! It was great to feel the movement of the ship again, but it promptly lulled me back to sleep. When I woke again at six I found we were alongside the wharf. Terrific!

I found the ship and the wharf ablaze with activity: such a contrast after the sloth of the past few days. We were tied up in Victoria dock, in a narrow berth only two ships wide, on wharf number three. The sacks of lentils were being lifted out of the holds by the ship's winches and dumped onto the deck, where Indian wharf labourers picked them up and carried them on their backs down the gangways to iron-wheeled handcarts on the wharf, where other men pushed them into the warehouse. The work of unloading went on feverishly almost all day and night. When the wharf labourers knocked off, scavengers appeared to pick up the spilled lentils.

28 The goddess of wealth

I went ashore for the first time in three weeks, still without a passport or visa, but with a seaman's shore pass stating that I was the Ship's Nurse of the *Pandora*. This enabled me to go ashore to visit but not stay; I couldn't check into a hotel without a passport or visa. I carried with me a shopping list from the rest of the crew, who were unable to land until unloading was finished.

A taxi, bearing the agent, pulled on to the dock, and I took it to the town, passing through the sentry post at the entrance to the wharf. I don't think they see a lot of ship's nurses, or female crew of any sort, these days. They certainly seemed surprised to see me.

The taxi took me to the Taj Mahal hotel. I wanted a breakfast to remember, and this was the best place in town, a marvellous edifice built in 1904 that stands tall on the foreshore of the bay. I changed some money into rupees, and parted with some of them for the privilege of indulging in a mountain of steak, eggs, fried potatoes, ham, sausages and fruit.

At peace with the world once more, I wandered outside and saw that I was finally in India.

The very name Bombay conjures exotic, romantic images of the days of the Raj, combined with all the mystery of the East. And, unlike Khartoum, the fantasy is not so far from the fact. Bombay was all I had imagined and more: a mixture of grand old Victorian buildings, exotic Indian temples, fine houses, slums, homeless beggars and millionaires. I found the beggars' plight distressing, but loved the vigour and colour of the crowded streets, markets and back-lanes. I had been afraid that the squalor and poverty would sadden me too much to enjoy the city, but there was much that was marvellous about Bombay.

A taxi took me to the Crawford Market, a kaleidoscope of sights and sounds in a massive, covered building constructed in 1867. Here everything conceivable is sold: meat, fish, cosmetics, fruit, vegetables, clothes, pots and pans, flowers, and even, so the ticket on the filing cabinet declared honestly, a 'vile cupboard'.

I was attracted to a display of brightly coloured packages, and tried to work out what they contained. Eventually the polite young man behind the stall said, 'Can I help you madam?' I replied, 'What are they?' 'Contraceptives, madam.' I dropped them like a hot coal and fled, to the enjoyment of the crowd of male onlookers. I had been a source of interest even before I provided this entertainment. There was no other white woman in sight and none of the local women seemed to go out alone.

I retreated to an eating house across the road to recover my composure and partake of more victuals. It was now about lunch time. The place had a café downstairs where the peasantry ate, but the higher caste were permitted to ascend the stairs to a 'finer' establishment (where doubtless the prices were double for the same food). I was ushered quickly up the stairs, I hope because I looked like gentry, and not because the owners thought it would bring down the tone of the place to have me seen from the street. Upstairs there was even more class distinction. I was led through a second-class place, a large dining hall, then finally allowed to come to rest in the hallowed air-conditioned room of the most elite. I was alone (perhaps their aim) in this, the ultimate feeding spot, and I had chop suey and ice-cream, although not together. The chop suey was nothing like it should be, but was tasty anyway, and the ice-cream was a solitary huge slab on a big dinner-plate. There were complimentary papadoms made with lentil or besan flour, a little dish of cardamom seeds to chew after eating to sweeten your breath, and a small serviette that on closer inspection revealed itself to be a folded square of toilet paper. All this splendour, air-conditioning, food and toilet paper cost less than a dollar. I knew then I was about to fall in love with India – it had lots of good food and was cheap.

I took a taxi back to the Taj, as it is known locally, to connect with the tour of the city I had booked for myself at breakfast. The bus arrived with only nine people doing their Well Behaved Tourist bit. It was the off season, and very hot and humid, but the bus wasn't air-conditioned. The guide was a lovely young female who smothered us with information. We crossed the causeway and passed the naval dockyard and the washerman's village with its regiments of laundry spread out to dry, then stopped at the Prince of Wales Museum with its natural history, art, archeological remains, miniature paintings, Buddha images and fantastic Oriental porcelain collection.

We proceeded on to the hanging gardens on top of Malabar Hill. The gardens are built on six inches of soil and cover what used to be the town reservoir. The reservoir was declared a non-event because the Towers of Silence, the Parsi burial site, were directly behind it. The Parsi dispose of their dead by placing them on top of high stone towers for the vultures to do away with.

Vultures are not renowned for delicate table manners and had a nasty habit of dropping bits of the dead, as well as their own excreta, in the town water supply, so it was thought a good idea to put the reservoir elsewhere. There are fantastic views from this high place, and the gardens over the old reservoir are very beautiful. Some of the credit is due to the vultures, no doubt, for fertilising the gardens instead of the water supply. We arrived at the Towers of Silence just as a body was being left there. The vultures were very much in evidence.

We scuttled away to the top of Malabar Hill, the highest part of Bombay, which afforded a spectacular view over the city and the curving bay edged with beaches of white sand and tropical greenery. Driving down from the hill again we visited the temple of the Jains, another of India's religious sects, where entry is forbidden to anyone wearing shoes. I added my sandals to the acre or so already under the eagle eye of an old woman who set herself up as the shoe guard and eked out a living from tips paid by people whose shoes remained unmolested. The temple, built of marble, was small but colourful, and had been erected in honour of the first Jain, Tirthankar Adinath. The entrance was flanked on either side by two half-sized statues of white elephants, complete with *mahout* – rider – and bright trappings. Inside, the temple was mirrored and painted in its entirety. Walls and ceilings were covered with decoration in vivid shades, mostly green-blue and turquoise, and the place was inhabited by a flock of statues similar to the Asian Buddha, but with Indian features and eyes.

The next stop was at 19 Laburnum Road, the house of Mahatma Ghandi, who was assassinated in 1947 as he led the struggle for Indian independence. It was a shrine. Even his spectacles were displayed as an objet for veneration.

We did not stop at the temple of Lakshmi, the goddess of wealth whose temple is the oldest in Bombay, but I made a note to return later and pay homage. Lakshmi seemed like a lady to get on the right side of. She is the wife of Vishnu the Preserver, the opposite deity of Shiva, the god of death.

Returning to the hotel I collected my parcels and took a taxi to a wine shop. These are the only places in Bombay where alcohol can be purchased by the bottle and they are not common. I bought provisions to restock the ship's bar and, from a street seller, a number of pretty peacock feather fans for the crew to take home to their wives, mothers or girl-friends. The merchant was a bedraggled boy, who looked as though he needed the money more than I did.

I arrived at the ship at dusk and was greeted like the prodigal returning. I certainly was bearing the equivalent of the fatted calf in seamen's eyes – booze. The crew worked on shifts until midnight, trying to get the cargo off as quickly as possible. The next morning the wharf was silent with that quiet Sunday feel. All the bustle of the previous day was gone, not because the workforce observes the Christian sabbath, but because the shed hands were on strike and the wharfies could not work without them. It was another idle day for the poor captain.

The ship was now definitely booked to collect a cargo in Sri Lanka, but the agent had convinced me that I should not go there and try to fly to Australia. There was serious strife in Colombo, with bombs going off daily in places like bus stations and airports. I agreed with him reluctantly and decided to fly home from India.

29 Country and eastern

That evening I arranged a Sailor's Night Out for the crew. Whenever I had asked Captain Pieter about paying something towards my fare he had replied, 'Take us out for a meal in Bombay.' So I did. In honour of the occasion I wore a new pink silk *khamis* suit I'd commissioned from an Indian tailor in Mombasa. *Khamis* suits are also called Pakistani suits, and consist of trousers that start out baggy at the hips and end up tight at the ankle, and a semi-fitting top which comes almost to the knees, with a split up both sides. They are comfortable to wear and solve a lot of the problems of dressing to suit the code of many countries. In Saudi I wore them under an *abeya*.

Our evening out started with a drink at the Ambassador, a revolving rooftop restaurant with a bird's-eye view over the city and the coast. It was dusk, and the lights along the coast were coming on. This string of coastal lights, known as the Queen's Necklace, is fabulous when seen from a height. The service in this establishment was only an afterthought to the view. They took half an hour to bring the first drink and gave us all the wrong orders so, when hunger pangs came upon us, we gave up on a second effort and proceeded by taxi to the Taj. The driver charged us treble the going rate, one of the drawbacks of travelling with a boatload of sailors. We dined at the famous Indian restaurant where the decor, the food – if you like hot Indian curry as much as I do – and the dancing girl were great, but the music dreadful country and eastern. A bottle of local wine cost eighty rupees, but imported wine was five to eight hundred rupees a bottle. We had the local. I had seen my companions ready to drink the medicinal alcohol in the first aid kit a few days earlier, and I was not going to pander to the palates of such as they. Captain Pieter had promised he would take me to a Low Seaman's Dive, but couldn't find one, so we went back to the ship, drank some port, spilled some, and went to bed.

Next afternoon I accompanied Pieter and Paul, the first engineer, to the agent's office, where I spent two hours trying to organise my visa while they did ship's business. The agent himself was an obliging man, who seemed to be doing his utmost to cut through the red tape for which India is famous, but I was not impressed with the travel department of his firm. The staff insisted that I had to get a visa for Australia, and no amount of my saying that I was an Australian, and therefore did not need one, could convince them otherwise. I decided to take my travel plans elsewhere.

At another agency I found a young woman in a becoming pale green sari, who helped me make a booking to Perth via Qantas. Pieter had told me to show them the seaman's home-leave ticket he had given me, and this got me a twenty-five per cent discount. It also permitted me a baggage allowance of forty kilos instead of the usual twenty. My leave pass said: 'The bearer of this letter is Lydia Laube who is presently signed on as a crew member of the MV *Pandora*, under the Dutch flag, and is being repatriated to Australia for leave.' But my ticket could not be given to me until I obtained an Indian visa, giving me permission to land in Bombay.

I set off down the street to explore. I was smiling at a street banner advertising a Car Rally for the Blind, when someone let off a long string of fire-crackers under my feet. I imagined a terrorist attack, and almost departed this world via a heart attack on the spot, but it turned out to be only a celebration of some sort. A passer-by kindly reassured me, 'It's not an exploiting bomb.'

It was almost time for me to leave ship – the ship's agent assured me that my visa was almost ready – and I spent the next morning looking for a suitable hotel. I found one I liked that was cheap, on the bay, with a nice view and clean, not a common virtue in Bombay for the money I was prepared to pay. I mentioned this place to the travel agent, and she threw up her hands in horror. 'You cannot stay there. It is only used by Arabs at night.' Saved again by the kind fates! The travel agent recommended a hotel in the suburbs at Kemp's Corner. I found it was small, but suitable, so I reserved a room for when I came ashore.

At the end of the day I still had received no news of my ticket or visa. The irony was that I only needed a visa for India in order to be able to leave it. I returned to the ship with some difficulty, remembering on the way back in the taxi that I had been awakened at first light by the sound of the ship's engines; we had been moving to another berth. Eventually I located her again on the Ballard Quay. On board I found the tailor who usually visited the ship when it was in port to gather orders for overalls or uniforms. This time he also whipped up a batch of *Pandora* T-shirts, hand embroidered with the ship's name and emblem. I still wear mine sometimes in memory of a great little ship.

30 I shall return

I received a message from the ship's agent telling me that he had secured me a temporary visa. He said he would disembark me and second officer Paul, who was going home to Holland on leave. He came at three and took us to customs. I bundled all my luggage in the taxi, and set off for fresh adventures.

I was not denied them. Customs formalities took three and a half hours and were a real experience. The customs people were used to dealing with sailors, and were flabbergasted by my jewellery list. They couldn't comprehend that all this loot was merely my personal effects, and seemed terrified that I was going to sell the lot and get them into awful trouble. The ironic thing was that, as I was over the permitted limit in cash and watches, I had these items secreted all over me – watches hidden on my arms under my sleeves in the time-honoured tradition, and money in my pockets under my jacket and other places which would necessitate a strip search to find. (I didn't think they would dare demand a formidable female like me display her pale hide.) I thought it should have appeared obvious, even to a government official, that if I intended to sell the jewellery I would not have declared it. My luggage was scrupulously searched, which struck me as a waste of time, seeing that I had already been stupid enough to state the cause of the problem to them. This customs scene began to remind me of Saudi Arabia. Here again was a room with seven people, behind seven desks, giving every indication that they had no other work this day with which to amuse themselves.

Another complication arose. The officials had managed to lose the form that had my camera and a few other items listed on it. They treated me politely, however, and seemed to be more confused than unkind. Two of the officers were women. One of them touched my arm and said, 'Oh! Look, what is this? There is something on your arm.' Oh, the wages of sin! I almost fainted with fright, thinking some of my contraband had escaped its concealment and was about to betray me. It would be prison for sure after all this. Looking down with my heart in my mouth, I saw a large smear of grease on my arm. I must have collected it during my exit from the ship.

My jewellery was dug out of my luggage and examined with interest, but it was obvious that the officials had no idea what it was worth. I should have described it as Woolworths junk and saved the bother. Eventually the senior person came up with the solution that all my jewellery would be confiscated and handed back to me at the airport as I left. Remembering their carelessness in losing one of my forms right before my eyes, I strongly resisted handing the jewellery over to them for 'safe-keeping'. It was a long way and a lot of red tape from here to the airport.

The officials decided to seek higher help. I was put in a taxi with two of them and taken to see the head of customs in down-town Bombay. We waited for an hour in the dim corridor of a crumbling old colonial building. To my relief, the head of customs was a woman. She swept into the room with a swish of blue silk sari. From behind me, neither looking at nor addressing me, she rapped out three short, sharp sentences and left. It was all over. The men, who had all leaped to their feet and stood to attention the whole time she was in the room, took me back to the wharf office. I think she told them they were damn fools to be making such a fuss. Something was said, rather sheepishly, in the taxi on the way back, about people at the airport knowing how to deal with this as they did it all the time. I certainly hope so. Otherwise what would it take to get a jumbo jet load of Americans through customs? We parted friends, with handshakes all round. Paul, who had been forced to wait through all this, and I were finally out.

We took a taxi to the hotel at Kemp's Corner, left my bags and went in search of refreshment. It was over four hours since we had left the ship and we were hot, thirsty and hungry. My hotel didn't have a restaurant, but the receptionist directed us to another hotel two doors down. We went into the bar for a drink. I don't think Indian women go to bars. I was the only woman in the place.

This establishment, which rejoiced in the romantic name of the Shalimar, seemed to be a meeting place for expatriates or Indians with western contacts or nostalgia for the Raj. An elderly, cultured Indian man introduced himself to us as Albert and said he was a journalist correspondent for the US *Star News*. He seemed to know everyone and before long so did we. One man said he bought wool from Australia. Someone else wanted to know if we had dollars for sale, so I sold some at a good rate. Another asked me what I knew about 'D Force'. I said 'Nothing whatsoever,' thinking he must be talking about some nasty new military weapon. It turned out he wanted to D Force his wife. At midnight I saw Paul away on his plane, returning happily to his bride of three months.

At the hotel I had a room the size of a cupboard, but

it was a very nice cupboard with a television, air-conditioner and a clean en suite bathroom. In the foyer I met an Indian poet who lived permanently at the hotel. He invited me into his rooms for tea, leaving the door open to observe the proprieties. I couldn't read his poetry as he wrote only in Hindi. Unfortunately he seemed to do a lot more drinking of the grape than he did poeting.

Accommodation in Bombay is dearer than elsewhere in India, possibly due to the many Arabs who come for holidays, but fortunately this is not the case with meals. I enjoyed many good curries and other local dishes. Lentil flour is much used in Indian cuisine, most enjoyably in *chappattis*, a flat, pancake-like bread. Tandoori chicken, marinated in yoghurt and spices and cooked in a special clay oven is delicious, as is *pomfret*, a fish like flounder, and Bombay duck, which is not a duck but a dried fish. *Pan*, which is betel nut and spices rolled into a quid for chewing, is taken after meals like brandy, and is mildly intoxicating and addictive. It also dyes your teeth red.

I lunched at the Shalimar with Albert, my journalist friend, and met an Australian veterinary surgeon who was in Bombay doing tests of a medicinal treatment he had invented. By an amazing coincidence he came from the same country town as I did, a dot in South Australia's mid-north that few have heard of.

I wandered around with a map, and found some fascinating markets, but at the Thieves' Market, *Chor Bazaar*, nothing was old or interesting. Either all the thieves in Bombay have reformed, or they only steal new stuff. I had no problem asking directions or being understood. Although Hindi is the major language, a large number of the people still speak English as a second language.

I was surprised to read in the local papers how extensively the trading in human flesh and organs still goes on in India. One article described the rescue of sixty women and children who had been taken by an international trafficking ring of slavers. The children would have been sold for sixty dollars each, and most of them then killed for organ transplants. The young women, who had been lured by offers of non-existent jobs, would have been sold for thirty dollars to brothels in India, Pakistan and the Middle East. Each year ten thousand women and children are listed as missing in India; most of them are never found.

The next day the *Pandora* was sailing for Colombo, so I took a taxi with Albert to see my friends off. It was no great surprise to find that their departure had been postponed for no apparent reason. We had lunch with the crew and left saying we would return at ten that night, their new time of leaving.

I went to the Shalimar for dinner. Craving some solitude, I chose the first-floor dining-room. Few people went there, most preferring to eat in the informal downstairs bar area. Later, I came here several times. I liked the way you could sit in front of the large open windows overlooking the street and watch India passing by below, or see it portrayed through the lighted but uncurtained windows of the apartments opposite. Looking down into the street, I saw an old woman with a basket of fodder on her head leading a cow on a rope against the traffic. Behind them came a younger woman with a milk bucket on her head. It was the fresh milk delivery service.

I was determined to see the ship off that evening. I met Albert and three of his photographer friends, who all said it wasn't safe for me to go alone to the wharf at night, and that they would accompany me. They found another friend who had a car, but he turned out to be very drunk. I was shepherded, against my protestations, into this man's tiny four-wheel-drive contraption, the others all squeezed in too, and there followed one of the most alarming rides of my life. The fellow drove as though we were on a race track. I have to admit, grudgingly, that he had considerable skill. Otherwise, drunk as he was, and he was much worse than I had thought at first, we would have been written off on the first bend. It was like being in one of those awful movie car chases. We shot through gaps between trucks with hair breadths to spare, dodged oncoming traffic like kamikaze pilots, and went around corners on two wheels. It was a very long half-hour drive to the wharf. I was seated between the two seats at the front next to the driver, with no seat under me and no seat-belt. I was staring death in the face the whole way and, to cap it all off the drunk, the horrible little man, decided he fancied me and took his hand off the wheel now and then to try to pat my thigh.

The ship had its gangplank up and I thought we were too late, but Hans, the second engineer, let it down and I tottered onboard, only to find that they were now sailing the next night at eleven. We stayed there for a while sobering up our driver. I insisted on riding in the back for the return trip, which at least foiled his dastardly designs on my person.

I set off next morning to find the Bendi Market and Mutton Street, the places where antique and junk shops rub shoulders. Here many relics of the Raj have come to rest, as well as some Oriental antiques. Much of it seemed to be inordinately expensive, but I bought a small brass betel box for a couple of dollars from a street stall. One of the dealers gave me his card which announced that he was Hanif who dealt in 'artful objects and curious' and gave his telephone number as 'Hello:34555'.

Back at the hotel I had a call from Raol, the first engineer on the ship, to say that they were sailing at ten that night – for sure this time. I went alone by taxi to the wharf, preferring the devil I didn't know to Albert's mate.

I found a large dark void where the *Pandora* had been. She must have gone early to catch the tide, or some peculiar Indian development had changed her plans. I stood there in the warm dark of a lovely night and felt lonely and homesick. I had lost, possibly for all time, my adopted home and family of the last four weeks. I had shared their lives and their work, listened to their worries and dreams, and now they were gone. This is one of the sorrows of being a traveller. Perhaps someday the *Pandora* will sail into some port where I am and we'll go looking for a low sailor's dive.

The day of my departure arrived. I went to the airport, which abounded with people of different nationalities, and passed uneventfully through to the departure lounge without anyone even asking for my customs declaration. I was miffed. I thought that after all the trouble I'd taken to get it organised, someone might at least have looked at it.

I was sorry to leave India. There was so much more to see and do. I could ride river boats and trains to strange places with extravagant names where new friends and fresh adventures awaited. Deciding to return one day, I boarded the plane and went home.

Also by Wakefield Press

BEHIND THE VEIL
An Australian nurse in Saudi Arabia
Lydia Laube

Lydia Laube worked as a nurse in a society that does not allow women to drive, vote or speak to a man alone. Wearing head to toe coverings in stifling heat, and battling administrative apathy, Lydia Laube kept her sanity and got her passport back.

Behind the Veil is the hilarious account of an Australian woman's battle against the odds. It will keep you entertained for hours.

ISBN 1 86254 267 8

SLOW BOAT TO MONGOLIA
Lydia Laube

Who else but Lydia Laube would climb the Great Wall of China waving a pink parasol while riding a donkey? In *Slow Boat to Mongolia* Lydia tells of her travels by ship, train and bone-shaking bus through Indonesia and China on her way to fabled Outer Mongolia.

Lydia learns to use chopsticks with aplomb and ploughs her way through crowds to visit places few westerners have ever seen. She reaches Outer Mongolia, where she stays in a *ger* in the snow and rides a horse through waist-high silvery grass.

ISBN 1 86254 418 2

Also by Wakefield Press

BOUND FOR VIETNAM
Lydia Laube

Lydia Laube never takes no for an answer. In *Bound for Vietnam*, against all protests, she finds ways to venture through rarely travelled parts of China, overcoming language barriers and standing her ground in crowded buses, boats and trains. She makes a meal of a snake and submits to the ministrations of the Dental Department of your worst nightmare.

Leaving China by pedal-power, Lydia enters Vietnam by motorbike and discovers a beautiful and resilient country.

Sit tight as you ride with our brave lone traveller. Her adventures will amaze and impress you.

ISBN 1 86254 462 X

LLAMA FOR LUNCH
Lydia Laube

In *Llama for Lunch*, Lydia Laube's latest adventure, she's off to South America in search of the sun.

Braving hair-raising mountainous tracks, bandits, immigration officials, jungle beasts and third-world dentists, she ventures through Mexico, down the Panama Canal, along the coast of Colombia, and into Peru, Bolivia and Brazil. Lydia explores the last hideaway of the Incas, Machu Picchu, and, fulfilling a lifelong dream, sails down the mighty Amazon to the Atlantic.

She travels alone into regions that armies of men would dare not enter – and, eventually, she learns how to catch the right bus.

ISBN 1 86254 576 6

Wakefield Press has been publishing good Australian books for over fifty years. For a catalogue of current and forthcoming titles, or to add your name to our mailing list, send your name and address to

Wakefield Press, Box 2266, Kent Town, South Australia 5071.

TELEPHONE (08) 8362 8800 FAX (08) 8362 7592
WEB www.wakefieldpress.com.au